RESILIENCE

RESILIENCE

How to Thrive Through Tough Times

GODFREY ESOH

Octave Books

Octave Books
An imprint of Njitamu Ventures LLC
201 Wickham Way, Apt 201, Norwood,
Massachusetts, 02062, USA.

Copyright © 2021 by Godfrey Esoh

All rights reserved. No part of this book may be reproduced in any manner whatsoever without written permission except in the case of brief quotations embodied in critical articles and reviews.

The information contained in this book is intended to be educational and not as a substitute for financial planning. This information should not replace consultation with a competent financial professional. The content of this book is intended to be used as an adjunct to a rational and responsible program prescribed by a financial professional. The author and publisher are in no way liable for any misuse of the material.

Published in the United States of America
ISBN: 978-1-7324517-2-8
ISBN: 978-1-7324517-3-5 (ebook)

First Printing, 2021

This book is lovingly dedicated to my late parents William and Regina whose resilience has been my best teacher.

Contents

Dedication   v

INTRODUCTION

1

PART 1: CULTIVATING RESILIENCE

1. Chapter 1: Understand Change   4
2. Chapter 2: Expect Change   11
3. Chapter 3: Prepare for Change   19
4. Chapter 4: Embrace Change   23
5. Chapter 5: Manage Change   28
6. Chapter 6: Grow With Change   31
7. Chapter 7: Lead the Change   39

2

PART 2: STORY OF A RESILIENT SOUL

8. Chapter 8: Rags to Riches   48
9. Chapter 9: Ugly War, Broken Dreams   58

10	Chapter 10: Walls in the Promised Land	72
11	Chapter 11: Black Lives Matter; My Life Matters	85
12	Chapter 12: An Apocalyptic Pandemic	92

3
PART 3: UNDERSTANDING AND MANAGING STRESS

13	Chapter 13: A Review of Human Needs	108
14	Chapter 14: The Origins of Stress	112
15	Chapter 15: How We Respond to Stress	124
16	Chapter 16: Be the Change	138

Introduction

I have been learning resilience for all the 40 years that I have been alive, and I have taught resilience for half of this time. As you will learn from the glimpses of my life journey presented in this book, not only was I born on the wrong side of the street, but I was born where there was no street at all. I had to make my own way as I went along, and by the time I was 20, I had been through so much and conquered so much that life had thrust me into a position of leadership and mentorship to others.

For the past 20 years, I have inspired and empowered millions of people through writing, speaking, coaching, and mentoring. The book you are about to read has evolved quite organically from the work I have been doing all these years both on myself and on the countless people I have helped to live happier and more abundant lives. For me, resilience is not just an academic subject or a trending topic for a business seminar. It is who I am. This is why this book is personal. It is easy to read and loaded with practical lessons and exercises that you can apply to your life. The book is divided into three parts:

In the first part of this book, I have laid out for you an 8 step formula for cultivating resilience: understanding change, anticipating change, preparing for change, welcoming change, managing change, growing with change, leading change, and being the change.

At the end of the book, I have included a chapter containing 15 exercises that you can systematically graft into your daily routine as you set out on your journey to cultivating resilience. Yes, resilience is a journey. There is no quick-fix formula for it. Thank you for being part of my journey, and thank you for using this book to become the more resilient person that the world needs.

The second part of this book gives you an immersive experience of the life of a child born into a humble family in a remote village in a remote town in a part of Africa that many people have never heard of. You will learn how this child braved several odds to become a community leader at the age of 17, a higher education administrator at the age of 26. You will learn how this hustler attained the summit of his career by winning an international award and getting appointed as Rector of a Polytechnic, only to leave it all behind and escape from war.

You will learn how this man was welcomed to America by the harsh reality of racism and an anti-immigrant government. You will learn how in the midst of the COVID-19 pandemic and all its socio-economic ramifications, this recent immigrant was not even eligible for a stimulus check. But more importantly, you will learn what it really means to be resilient in the face of your own challenges.

The third part of this book is a reflection about our human needs and why it is crucial for our human needs to be satisfied in a balanced way. This section helps you get a better understanding of how stress arises as a result of unmet needs. Finally, you will learn how most mental health issues, relationship woes, financial hardships, and career misfortunes are linked to a negative adaptation to stress.

1

Part 1: Cultivating Resilience

"Resilience is knowing that you are the only one who has the power and the responsibility to pick yourself up."
~Mary Holloway~

I

Chapter 1: Understand Change

Living in today's world is like flying in an aircraft that is experiencing turbulence. Everyone needs to have their seatbelt on. Everyone needs to know where the life jacket is and how to put it on. Everyone needs to know where the exits are located. Yes, the turbulence in the world is shaking the core of life as we know it. Financial systems are being disrupted, educational systems are being disrupted, religious systems are being disrupted, political systems are being disrupted, and the way in which we live life as individuals and communities is being disrupted. But there is no need to panic.

The change we are experiencing is the birth pangs of a new dawn for humanity. The key is to understand change so that we can manage it and emerge on the other side as transformed beings rather than as victims. That is what resilience is about.

Understand that the universe is a living system that is in a state of perpetual expansion. This force by which life unfolds in our universe evolution. It expresses itself in different ways and on different scales. As part of this universe, you are like a passenger in a moving spaceship. Life is always changing, and you are always changing with it.

Understand that change unfolds in cycles. Just as we have, day, night, summer, fall, winter, and spring, everything else in the universe is subject to cyclical changes.

Understand that society also evolves according to trends. Not long ago we were living in the agrarian age. Then came the industrial revolution. Then followed the computer revolution. When the internet revolution came, we thought we had seen it all. Now we have the social media, cloud computing, and crypto revolutions. What is coming next and how will it change the way we live?

Understand that natural disasters and conflicts do occur. While natural disasters are the manifestation of planetary shifts and climate change, conflicts are the manifestation of social shifts. These forces have been with us since life began on our planet and they will continue to be. Just like a surfer knows how to navigate a wave and actually take advantage of it, your role in the face of change is to know how to prevent it from destroying you, and rather leverage its power for good.

Understand that people change. Because people change, our relationships are bound to change. Because people change, our communities are bound to change. Because people change, our work environments and businesses are bound to change.

Understand that you too are changing. As a human being, your life also unfolds according to a human life cycle. At various stages of that cycle, your needs and priorities are different. At various stages of that cycle, your mental and emotional dispositions are different. At various stages of that cycle, your immunity and physical resilience are different.

Be a deliberate creator

Most people do not get what they want in life because most people do not know what they really want in life. Most people do not know what they really want in life because they have been socially programmed to chase illusions rather than concrete goals.

For example;

MONEY is not an object that you can chase and catch. Money is the transactional energy or value current that flows to you as a result of the value you create in your environment. To receive money, you must BE valuable and GIVE value. You do not get money by paying tithes and sowing seeds in church. If your tithes and seeds are good enough, you will receive an inspired idea that you need to act on. Heaven will never drop money into your laps no matter how holy you are.

HAPPINESS is not an entitlement that the people in your life are supposed to give you. Happiness is a state that you awaken within your soul when you are busy creating happiness for others. To receive happiness, you must BE happy and GIVE happiness. You do not get happiness in your marriage or relationship by fasting and praying novenas. If your fasting and praying is good enough, they will open your eyes to see the people in your life that you need to forgive and serve.

LOVE is not a trophy that you pursue and acquire. Love is the blossoming of that heart that is busy pouring itself out selflessly for others. To receive love, you must BE love and GIVE love. You do not get love by speaking in tongues and reciting affirmations. If your tongues and affirmations are of any merit, they will inspire you to open your heart and start being the love that you expect to get.

SUCCESS is not an object that you can chase and catch. Success is the state of abundance and wellbeing that surrounds you when you are busy being a self-actualized person through the practice of the spirit of excellence. To receive success, you must BE abundant and GIVE abundance. Success will not come to you because you visualized and believed. If your visualizing and believing actually works, it will spur you to acquire the knowledge, skill, and attributes that you will put to work through a deliberate and organized strategy to achieve a clearly defined goal.

Here are some keys that can help you to stop chasing illusions and start living your authentic life:

1. Know your authentic self
2. Take responsibility and decide the life you want
3. Find your passion and turn it into your career
4. Find a massive problem to solve
5. Prepare for success by investing in yourself
6. Create a unique solution for a starving market
7. Give more value than the reward you receive
8. Begin each day with excitement
9. End each day with gratitude
10. See money as the happy shadow of your indispensable value
11. Never stop growing; keep shifting the boundaries of your comfort zone
12. Always have your legacy in mind

With a little self-reflection, you can find ways to put these 12 keys into practice. When your spirit, soul, mind, and body are totally immersed in the act of actually living life, all the other things will flourish on you like the leaves that grow on a tree that is planted by the riverside. Money will follow you like a shadow, happiness will be as constant as your breath, love will cover you like a fragrance. That is what I call, spontaneous success.

In order to be a deliberate creator, you must know who you truly are.

The fundamental problem of life is that most human beings do not know who they are. Why do most human beings not know who they are? Because we are subconsciously programmed to be the image of the environment that raised us. Look at it this way:

Schools, churches, and governments do not teach us how to be rich. Where then do we learn about money? We learn about money in our homes and communities. So, if 95% of humans are broke, it means that 95% of human beings learn about money from poor people. What will be the effect on society? 95% of the people will always inherit poverty from the 95% of broke people who raise them.

Schools, churches, and governments do not teach us how to love. Where then do we learn about love? We learn about love in our homes and communities. So, if 95% of humans are self-centered, it means that 95% of human beings learn about love from self-centered people. What will be the effect on society? 95% of the people will always inherit self-centeredness from the 95% of self-centered people who raise them.

Schools, churches, and governments do not teach us how to be happy. Where then do we learn about happiness? We learn about happiness in our homes and communities. So, if 95% of humans are miserable, it means that 95% of human beings learn about happiness from miserable people. What will be the effect on society? 95% of the people will always inherit misery from the 95% of miserable people who raise them.

Schools, churches, and governments do not teach us how to excel in life. Where then do we learn about success? We learn about success in our homes and communities. So, if 95% of humans are mediocre, it means that 95% of human beings learn about success from mediocre people. What will be the effect on society? 95% of the people will always inherit mediocrity from the 95% of mediocre people who raise them.

What then is the bottom-line? Our answer can be found in the timeless inscription at the entrance to the Temple of Luxor in Ancient Egypt; "Man, know thyself".

But what does it really mean to know yourself? We know practically nothing about the inspired messengers who inscribed these words at the entrance of the ancient temples before recorded history. But there is something I know for sure. What these words mean is that you need to lift the veil of the false self you have been carrying around, so that you can dispel the illusion of the false reality that this false self has been creating.

You do not need to get rich because you have never been poor. Poverty is an illusion of the false self you have been carrying around. The only wealth you need is to wake up to the realization of your true identity.

You do not need a secret to success because you have never been a failure. Failure is an illusion of the false self you have been carrying around. The only success you need is to wake up to the realization of your true identity.

Your authentic identity is that hidden treasure that once you find it in a certain field, you will need to go and sell everything you have to come and buy that field.

Holistic Health

Holistic health is the state of balance that we seek. While it is impossible for a human being to have all his/her needs adequately met at a given point in time, life is a dynamic process that will maintain an overall state of health if the various components are balanced. According to the Afrocentric paradigm of reality, a balanced person is a spiritual entity who possesses emotional and mental faculties with which he/she operates a physical body through which he/she interacts with the environment, as part of a community.

Taking all these components into consideration (spirit, soul, mind, body, environment, and community) is crucial if the state of holistic health is to be attained.

2

Chapter 2: Expect Change

When you expect people to change, you will learn to be more flexible with your expectations of people. When you expect people to change, you will approach their change with empathy and learn to see life from their perspective than from your selfish needs. When you expect people to change, you will avoid unnecessary stress and shock when those changes occur.

When you expect your career to change, you will become aware of the need to continue investing in life-long learning and personal empowerment. This is the only way to make sure that when change arrives, you are ready for it.

When you expect your finances to change, you will see the need to cultivate the habit of saving or unplanned expenses. It does not matter how much you make. What makes you rich is how much you get to keep. In one instant, that job or business can disappear. A war may break out, a pandemic may occur, a lockdown may come, a natural disaster may show up, an accident may happen, a prolonged illness or disability may occur. You don't want these, but it is wiser to have a backup that you never use than not have one and then wake up one day and be in need of it when it is too late.

When you expect your health to change, you will see the wisdom in heaving a good health and life insurance policy. Being aware that what you eat and do today affects your health tomorrow will also help you stay more conscious about what you eat and do.

When you expect social changes to occur, you will include in your life plan, the readiness to make some radical changes if the need arises. For example, moving to another town or another country could be the most viable option in the face of conflict or some deep personal loss. But this option is open to you only if you have the means to move. And you will have the means only if you were prepared.

Look Within

Most people attribute the results in their lives to external causes with which they have a relationship that is fundamentally superstitious. They attribute the good things to an external God whom they need to cajole for blessings through religious prayers, and rituals. They attribute the bad things to an external devil whose hand they see in ancestral spirits or enemies.

For those who are not traditional or religious, the government and other external circumstances are the scapegoats. A classic demonstration is the 40 million Americans who are now unemployed and are blaming it on COVID-19, not to mention the over half a billion Africans who blame their poverty on their governments and colonial past. Lazy and irresponsible people always find someone else to blame for their troubles so that they can shift responsibility for action to that person or power. They want change, so long as it is someone else that needs to change or make the change happen.

I am in no way claiming that these external forces are unreal. What I am emphasizing is that if you cultivate the victim attitude, you will always find someone or something to blame. But if you choose to cultivate the conquering spirit instead, you will always find ways of taking responsibility and making the change happen. Why is it that while some people are losing their jobs, others are starting businesses? Why is it that while some people are going without food, others are becoming billionaires? Your attitude determines how you adjust to a crisis, and it is the kind of adjustment that culminates in either happiness or misery.

The superstitious and escapist approach to life, no matter how pious it may appear, is the symptom of primitive souls that have refused to evolve. Change is the only constant thing in this world. Change is the force of evolution. Change is painful only when we do not understand it. Let me now introduce you to the Law of Gestation, a system of natural principles that you can use to prepare a blueprint for your life, adopt a scientific approach to any goal, and ascertain the success of any venture.

SEED STAGE

Every reality in our physical universe began as an idea in the mind of the Creator. Every invention, every discovery, every accomplishment, was first a thought in the human mind. Every life form has an embryonic stage. The desire in your heart is the seed of your future. But a seed will never turn into a harvest without passing through the various stages involved in the law of gestation. Forget about superstitious beliefs and religious prayers. To know the law and corporate with the law is to work with God. When you work with God (law), your results are certain, predictable, and inevitable.

SOWING STAGE

When a fertile male mates with a fertile female, sowing takes place in the womb of the female. This is what is known as fertilization. The male sperm fuses with the female egg to form an embryo. The farmer who wants to harvest corn knows that she must sow corn seeds into the ground and cultivate that ground. The person who seeks to become rich must also know that riches will come to him only as a result of finding a product or service through which he can render value to a multitude of people who have a burning need and desire for it.

INCUBATION STAGE

Incubation is the "dark night of the soul" during which it feels like nothing is happening. Your seed dies and remains buried in the ground for several weeks, months, or even years. On its journey to becoming a butterfly, the caterpillar goes through a period of death or pupation. You look at the cocoon and wonder what is going on, but there is nothing you can do to skip or accelerate the incubation phase. If you do not allow it to follow its natural course, you will end up with a dead or malformed butterfly. The lack of evidence of growth gets some people so impatient that they are tempted to dig up their seed and see what is happening. When they give in to this temptation, they destroy the miracle of life. all those who give up on their dreams and projects do so at the incubation stage because they did not understand the life cycle of the venture they were pursuing.

BIRTH STAGE

When the embryo is fully formed, the miracle of birth occurs. When a life form is born into the world, that is when everyone sees and interacts with it and marvels at it. What most people do is that they take their seed, announce it to the world, ask for people's opinions about it, and even ask for permission from their friends, authorities, and loved ones. By exposing their seeds, they have moved to the delivery stage without passion through the sowing and incubation stage. What do you expect? The seed is bound to experience a steel birth. It is the law. You cannot turn a sperm cell into a healthy child without first fertilizing a woman's egg with it and incubating it in the womb. Whether it is money you want, whether it is a business you are building. Whether it is a relationship you are cultivating, the law is universal and cannot be broken.

GROWTH STAGE

When a child is born and turns the home into a celebration mood; when a crop germinates and turns the farm green; when a business is launched and you feel a sense of accomplishment; when you secure your dream job and receive that first paycheck, you must remember that there is still something called "growth". You need to nurture your new baby by investing in it all that is required to groom it into the best version of itself possible. The salary you receive from your job or the profit you make from your small business is not what will make you reach. This is capital. If you eat all of it, you have aborted your dreams. If you invest it, you will grow your wealth.

MATURITY STAGE

We say that a human is mature when it is mentally, physically, emotionally, and socio-economically capable of bringing forth another human life. Although most women are biologically capable of getting pregnant by the age of 12 and most men are biologically capable of impregnating a woman by the age of sixteen, there is a good number of humans who even at 40, cannot be said to be mature because their minds, emotions, and socio-economic situations have not yet caught up with their biology.

What are the unique knowledge, skills, experiences, and networks that you have cultivated that make you an indispensable value creator in your environment? The simple formula for wealth is this;

"the amount of money you earn will always be in direct proportion to the need for what you do, your ability to do it, and the difficulty there is in replacing you". What you have or don't have is what you have earned. Yes, you deserve more, but your ignorance may have prevented you from doing what needs to be done to earn it. God has nothing to do with it, the devil has nothing to do with it, your ancestors have nothing to do with it, and there is no enemy anywhere that is sabotaging your progress, apart from the one inside your head.

HARVEST STAGE

The greatest disservice that humans do to themselves is that they spend all their time focusing on results instead of the process that engenders the results. Instead of fasting, praying, paying tithes, affirming, and wishing to be like Oprah Winfrey, Aliko Dangote, Mother Teresa, Nelson Mandela, Bill Gates, or Jeff Bezos, focus your energies on understanding these people's respective journeys and the chain of causality that led to the results you are now observing. When you immerse yourself in the stories of the people you look up to, you enter into the spirit of their lives.

When you enter into the spirit of their lives, you awaken in you the capacity to mentally reverse engineer their chain of causality and then graft into your unique story the elements that can make you a brand new version of those people. Don't be a fan. Don't be a follower. Be a student. Perform mental reverse engineering on your role models, then become a unique version of them. Every effect follows a cause. If you create the cause, the effect will be inevitable.

EXPANSION STAGE

What would happen to the mango species if a mango seed were to grow into a mango tree, bear a thousand fruits, then die without endowing those fruits with the capacity to give birth to other mango trees? Certainly, the mango species will get extinct. Nature teaches us the law of propagation or multiplication so that we can have daily reminders that no matter how successful, great, rich, and influential you become, your life counts for nothing if you do not leave a legacy.

Apply the four-generation rule. If you are building a house, build a house that will still appear new by the time your great-grandchildren are born. If you are building a business, build a business that your great-grandchildren will grow and inherit. When thinking about money, do not think about the peanuts that you require to pay for your house, car, and survival needs; build a system that will guarantee generational wealth. One of the dumbest prayers I was raised to recite every day is this "Give us this day our daily bread". You condition your mind for daily bread for your 60 years of being a Christian, and then you die wondering why someone else owns the bakery and someone else owns the plantation on which the wheat grows.

***

Over the past half-century, the world has paid dearly for the multibillion-dollar lies called motivation, law of attraction, positive thinking, and so on. The law of attraction is the mechanism by which Effects follow Causes. If you order an item online and key in your home address, your parcel will find you where you are, thanks to the orchestration of the courier services. That is what the law of attraction is – it is a delivery service. You cannot mediate yourself into a fortune with the law of attraction.

In the same vein, people who need external help to think positively and feel motivated are people who do not really want what they are pretending to be wanting. Having a dream is like falling in love. If it does not kick you out of bed in the morning and keep you fired up all day, then you are wasting your time just being busy. Can you take one goal in your life and write out a blueprint for it using the law of gestation that I have taught you?

Chapter 3: Prepare for Change

There is great truth to the saying that "the best defense is attack". Change is a constant force of nature, and the degree to which you become stressed by change is a reflection of how unprepared or how prepared you were for change. If you understand that change is the only constant thing in life, and you become accustomed to expecting change, the only thing that will keep you sane is the assurance that you are prepared for any change that may come.

So, how do you prepare for change? You cannot micro-manage change because you are not the one causing the change, and for the most part, you have no clue about what particular change is coming. Therefore, the best way to prepare for change is to stop focusing on external factors and give your attention to the one thing that is within your control – you. Resilience is about transforming yourself into a person that does not only survive but thrives through change. Here is how you can become resilient and antifragile.

Prepare yourself spiritually by becoming more aware of the transcendent essence that constitutes the real you. That is, the formless presence that is experiencing your identity, emotions, thoughts, body, and circumstances. Spiritual Awareness is no respecter of religion, and the fact that it is not taught in school does not make it less important. Without a spirituality, you are like a house built on shifting sand. Find a spiritual practice that is conducive to your makeup and really immerse yourself in it.

Prepare yourself emotionally through the practice of self-contemplation. Observe the identity from which you are living your life, observe the emotions that flow from that identity, examine the processes through which this identity and emotions have been conditioned, then learn how to reprogram yourself into the version of you that you do want.

Prepare yourself mentally by educating yourself. The more knowledgeable you are, the broader your worldview. The broader your worldview, the clearer your paradigm or mental lens. The clearer your paradigm, the more choices you have in life. There is no greater treasure than wisdom.

Prepare yourself physiologically by taking care of your body. Realize that you are a conscious being that is navigating the universe with the help of your body vehicle. The quality of experiences that you can enrich your life with depends on the ability of your body to process those experiences. So, you must stay healthy, fit, and happy.

Prepare yourself socially by surrounding yourself with people that empower you, people that you can count on when the going gets tough, and people that protect you from your worst instincts. Don't just grow and die where you were born like a tree. Choose the environment in which you will be proud to build your home, raise your children, and grow old.

The Value of a Support Community

Stress is not a personal issue. Stressed individuals are symptomatic of a stressed society. The only genuine remedy for stress is a balanced society that values humans and celebrates life. The modern world has built a capitalistic society that values money, celebrates power, and uses humans. The good news is that you do not need to wait for the world to change before you can change. Rather, you can contribute to changing the world by beginning to change your life.

Begin where you are to build a community of love. We need communities of love, not therapy or support groups. There is a world of difference between the two. Therapy groups work on the premise that you are sick, weak, and needy. Although they benefit people in the short-run, they are indeed disempowering and in the long-term constitute part of the problem.

A community of love is a totally different concept that changes the conversation by flipping the paradigm. We are strong, we are amazing, we are great, we are sufficient, and we thrive by bringing out the best in one another. When communities of love emerge everywhere, we will eventually have the critical mass that will cause a massive shift in society.

Some Stress Prevention Exercises

Following are some self-help stress relievers that you can incorporate into your daily routine to get your stress under control:

- Trying meditation, yoga or deep breathing
- Getting regular physical activity
- Getting enough sleep
- Eating a healthy diet
- Managing your time
- Cutting back on obligations

Steps in stress self-management

The National Institute of Mental Health recommends the following ways to manage stress:

Recognize the Signs of your body's response to stress, such as difficulty sleeping, increased alcohol and other substance use, being easily angered, feeling depressed, and having low energy.

Talk to Your Doctor or Health Care Provider. Get proper health care for existing or new health problems.

Get Regular Exercise. Just 30 minutes per day of walking can help boost your mood and reduce stress.

Try a Relaxing Activity. Explore stress coping programs, which may incorporate meditation, yoga, tai chi, or other gentle exercises. For some stress-related conditions, these approaches are used in addition to other forms of treatment. Schedule regular times for these and other healthy and relaxing activities.

Set Goals and Priorities. Decide what must get done and what can wait, and learn to say no to new tasks if they are putting you into overload. Note what you have accomplished at the end of the day, not what you have been unable to do.

Stay Connected with people who can provide emotional and other support. To reduce stress, ask for help from friends, family, and community or religious organizations.

Seek professional help right away if you have suicidal thoughts, are overwhelmed, feel you cannot cope, or are using drugs or alcohol to cope.

Chapter 4: Embrace Change

You welcome change by practicing non-resistance. We resist when we feel deficient, insecure, uncertain, and afraid. But when we understand change, expect change, and prepare for change, there is no need to resist change.

- Detaching from the past frees you from regrets
- Detaching from the future frees you from fears
- Detaching from circumstances frees you from worry
- Detaching from information overload, conspiracy theories, media propaganda, and negative people frees you from panic and anxiety
- When you are free from regrets, fears, worry, and anxiety, you will find it natural to be fully present in the moment.

Learn resilience from water.

For as long as I can remember, my life has been so rocky that almost every turn I have made in life, I have first had to hit a wall. My need to outgrow my limited past was stronger than the pain and humiliation I felt, so I never stopped. Whenever life slapped me in the face, I simply looked for another way. Eventually, my life became like a meandering stream. I never used to realize why I love walking along the banks of streams, but now I get it.

The stream is a perfect mirror of my life. When the flowing water comes across an obstacle, it does not turn back or sit there complaining. It meanders its way around it. If it is dammed on all sides, it patiently fills up until it can flow above the obstacle. This is how water, the softest substance you can think of, turns out to be the toughest substance in reality. You can't break it because it can bend itself into any shape that you create. That is resilience at its finest. Your ability to welcome change is the key to becoming as resilient as water.

The author, speaker, mentor, and coach that I have become happened totally by accident. It was a result of my resilience in the face of my personal struggles. I gave my first speech because I graduated on top of my class and after that discovery, speaking became a part of me. I started journaling as a personal healing process and the moment I had the courage to start sharing my meditations, things just exploded. People started coming to me for help as a result of the insights they were reading from my publications, and before I knew it, I had practiced personal coaching and mentoring for twenty years.

It is only when I got to the USA that it dawned on me that what I had been practicing as a hobby for two decades was actually a career that could have a global consequence. It is because of this realization that you now have this book in your hands. And it all happened because I have always welcomed change.

What started as an innocent hobby several years ago has grown through persistent and habitual practice to become a fire of inspiration that is lighting up the world. From the year 2000 when I started delivering Sunday Reflections in the University of Buea Catholic Community, through 2009 when I started publishing on Facebook, through 2018 when I launched the Godfrey Esoh Inspiration daily series on WhatsApp, I have written and published a minimum of 1000 inspirational articles that have reached millions of people. Between 2018 and 2019 alone, I published for over 400 days without ever skipping a day.

Thanks to the feedback I regularly receive from readers in Cameroon, Nigeria, South Africa, India, Germany, United Kingdom, Sweden, Canada, The United States, The United Arab Emirates, and Thailand, I know that my work has now gone global. In fact, last year, I developed an entire course that an NGO is using as part of their innovative work in tackling mental health issues among rural youths in India.

I gave my first public speech as valedictorian of my class during our graduation from Primary School in 1992. This experience sowed a seed that germinated in Secondary School when I used to thrill the staff and students during morning assembly as a reporter for The Journalism Club. My five years' experience as Class Prefect helped me build confidence in standing up and talking among people, even when I had to communicate 'bad news' to a not-too-friendly group of students. By the time I became President of the Mbatu Students' Association in 1998, I had already matured as a public speaker.

In 2016, in the beautiful city of Port Elizabeth, the hometown of Nelson Mandela, I received my induction into the global scientific community when I mounted the stage to deliver my first international scientific presentation at an international conference. The following year, 2017 I sat on a distinguished panel with five other colleagues from South Africa, Uganda, Uruguay, India, and the Philippines, where together, we presented to the medical education community the innovative ideas with which we had won the "Projects That Work" award.

This award took place in Hammamet, Tunisia, during the first-ever world summit on Social Accountability in Medical Education, and I was privileged to be one of the 450 delegates from 40 countries (the only one from Cameroon) who participated in giving to the world, "The Tunis Declaration".

In March 2018, I was invited as a panelist during the "Africa's Brain Bank Summit" in Maryland, USA, and a month later, I graced the fundraising event of a USA-based NGO as a guest speaker.

1998 to 2018 is a span of 20 years, and in these twenty years, I attained the pinnacle of influence, doing something that I have always done simply as a hobby. In this fact, lies the secret that I want to reveal to you today.

"Time is a compounding factor, a law of growth that silently but unfailingly multiplies the seed of habit you sow into it."

If you look at your life, you will realize that the results you are manifesting in every area are the compound interest you are reaping from the savings you have been cultivating in the form of your habits in that domain. Be it your health, relationships, career, finances, business, or spiritual life, the quality of your results is the compound interest that time is paying back to you for the habits of thinking, feeling, speaking, and doing that you have been systematically sowing into your life over the years.

If you acquaint yourself with the new scientific concepts of neuroplasticity, neurochemistry, epigenetics, and biofields, you will see that the process through which your life experience unfolds is purely scientific. This understanding will stop you from running helter-skelter looking for deliverance from men of God or village shrines, or for rapid success strategies from motivational seminars and books. They are all scams. Only you can change yourself, and you change yourself by changing yourself. Do you like the way this sounds? Only you can change yourself, and you change yourself by *changing yourself.* You cannot pray or wish it into being.

It is small habits that the power of time compounds into big results. Therefore, how the big results come about is none of your concern. The law of growth takes care of that. Your job is to become aware of those habits you innocently practice on a daily basis. Choose the ones that are helping you build a better life and engage them more deliberately. Take note of the ones that are killing you and begin replacing them with constructive ones.

Success is as simple as knowing who you want to be, being aware of the habits you are practicing, and disciplining yourself to religiously practice the habits that will transform you in the long run into the person you want to become.

Chapter 5: Manage Change

"In a world of change, the learners shall inherit the earth, while the learned shall find themselves perfectly suited for a world that no longer exists." ~Eric Hoffer~

Manage yourself by practicing self-awareness, understanding stress, and mastering how to prevent and manage stress.

Manage people by understanding the personality types of the people you have a relationship with and making an effort to respond to them with empathy.

Manage career and business changes by identifying and leveraging the new opportunities that arise when old systems crumble.

Manage financial changes by reviewing your budget and streamlining your expenses. Delayed gratification is rewarding when you have better days to look forward to.

Manage social change by accepting that there are things that are beyond your control. Keep a cool head and look for the trends that are emerging and that you can factor into your adjustment plan.

Understand inertia, then conquer it.

When people become used to a habitual way of thinking, speaking, and acting, that habit becomes a tradition. A tradition is a paradigm, a stereotype, a belief system, a social conditioning that is lodged in the subconscious mind. It is the mental software that automatically controls the lives of people even when they are not aware of it. 95% of the activities that the average human being or organization performs on a daily basis is accounted for by this law of habit. Self-preservation is a basic instinct that all living things have, and tradition is a mode of self-preservation.

When we say that people are resistant to change, it is not entirely true. The real truth is that people are afraid of being changed. They would have no problem with the change you effect on yourself, your work, or your community if that change was not going to force them to change. If your actions are going to cause people to change the way they do their own work, go about their own lives, relate with you and others, then they will resist you. You will often notice at your job site that when you are a super-performer, you make your colleagues and bosses uncomfortable.

This is not usually because they envy you. It is rather because by being a super-performer, you are raising the performance bar of the organization, and by so doing, exposing their mediocre routine and forcing them to change and catch up with you. If you are a peak performer, never expect your office to be a comfort zone. Your good work will instead make people backstab and crucify you on a daily basis. If you know this, you will prepare for it and face this challenge differently.

Remember the second law of motion, the law of inertia, which says that an object in motion will continue in uniform motion in the same direction while an object at rest will continue to stay at rest until acted upon by an external force. You need to see yourself as that external force that needs to act against the resistance that peoples' comfort zones create. You can act on people either by being a fire of inspiration that sets their souls ablaze, or by creating some new product, service, strategy, or system that kicks them in the butt, gives them no choice, and renders the old one obsolete.

When Obama set out to be America's first black president, he knew what he was bargaining for. When great innovators like Steve Jobs, Bill Gates, and Jeff Bezos set out to revolutionize the way humans live their lives, they knew what they were bargaining for. By knowing the resistance that they would face and preparing for it beforehand, innovators make dealing with challenges part of their daily work. the average human on the other hand spends most of their energy complaining, blaming, playing the victim, and reacting to circumstances.

You will dramatically transform your relationship, your finances, your career, and whatever you are involved in, if you become a master of change. Anticipate change, and move with the change.

6

Chapter 6: Grow With Change

If you perceive change as a force of transformation, then it will become clear to you that there is no such thing as a return to normal. We are always evolving from one new normal to another. What this means is that those who move ahead in life are those who grow with change, not those who merely survive change. You grow with change by;

Acquiring new knowledge that empowers you to understand the change you are living in and the opportunities that come with it.

Cultivating new skills that you can use to create new products or services, or transform your current job or business.

Developing new abilities with which to respond to your changing personal reality, relationships, communities, work environments, and business.

Building new networks and communities that provide the support system you need to thrive, such as teachers, mentors, coaches, mastermind groups, peer groups, and clients.

Practicing new habits or strategies that are in alignment with the new results you want to see in your personal life, health, relationships, finances, and career.

Build your life in changeless principles.

Do not panic. Stay calm. Know that the storms will pass. Base your life on a solid set of principles you can apply on a consistent basis in any weather, with the assurance that the turbulence will pass and you will emerge victoriously.

If you grew up in the village and spent your childhood helping your mother on the farm, this will come as a surprise to you. Yes, it is surprising that the greatest wisdom in the universe has been locked up in your body unused for all these years. You have been fooled into treasuring the classroom lectures and the school certificates, and you have failed to realize that there is no amphitheater, no professor, no textbook, that can teach you anything more valuable than the education that was systematically programmed into your cells by nature itself.

My mother, Manwing Regina Kieng, who never had as much as a Primary school report card, remains the most revered professor in my life, and I am about to show you why. God reveals Himself in strange ways, and "The 12 Fundamental Laws of Success", which I learned through my interaction with my mother in the farm, is clearly one of those strange ways.

Let us examine how nature reveals its secrets through the farm, and how our life is just like the farm.

LAW #1: A SOLID FOUNDATION
Every village woman has her farm that she identifies with as the

source of livelihood for her household. She has her farming tools and farm basket with which she interacts with her farm. She has a lifestyle that boils down to a predictable relationship with her farm. Every life needs to be solidly grounded in a sense of identity and purpose. Every person is supposed to be actively pursuing their purpose through a specific career. Success is supposed to be a lifestyle.

LAW #2: DELIBERATE CREATION

Different types of crops do well on different types of soils. So, you know where to plant yams, where to plant corn, and where to plant vegetables. It is the same with your life. Your health, your career, your relationships, your finances, etc., all combine to make up a successful life but each one must be nurtured in a unique way. For each area of your life to flourish, you need to consciously identify the need, intentionally choose the change, then cultivate the specific combination of specialized knowledge, skills, and attitudes that are unique to that domain. Success does not just happen; it is the result of deliberate creation.

LAW #3: RHYTHM

There is a season to sow and a season to reap. If you do not sow during the planting season, you will wind up as a beggar or at best spend a lot of money on what others are enjoying for free. There is a time to work and a time to enjoy; there is a time to invest and a time to reap the profits. Your youth is the planting season of your life and your adulthood is the harvesting season. You will enjoy in later life if only you sowed in your youth. If you waste the sowing season trying to use shortcuts to reap fruits that are meant for a different season, it will not be long before you will find yourself bankrupt in both material and immaterial things.

LAW #4: PREPARATION

Before sowing, you must clear the bush, till the soil, and prepare the ground. Same thing in real life. You cannot think, talk, pray, and wait for miracles. You must get your hands dirty, sweat it out, and do some work. Prayer is for revelation, but actualization takes work. You must cleanse your mind of the limiting stereotypes that have been programmed into you by society; you must cultivate the specialized knowledge and skills needed to succeed, then you must get busy.

LAW #5: CORRESPONDENCE

The quality of the seed you sow determines the quality of harvest you get. So commonsense demands that you select the very best seeds. Also, the specific seed you sow determines the specific crop you harvest. It is impossible to plant yams and harvest potatoes. In life, your audacious goals and your commitment to excellence represent the good seeds. Small goals stimulate mediocre effort and mediocre effort engenders mediocre results. Mighty goals inspire massive inspired action, and massive inspired action engenders excellent results. The law of identical harvest can never be broken.

LAW #6: GROWTH

After preparing the best soil and sowing the best seed, you wait on the law of growth to do its part. You do not dig up the seed every morning to see what is happening to it. You trust in that power that is greater than you to convert your seed into a harvest because it must be so by the law of creation. It has nothing to do with what you think or say or believe. The law must fulfill itself. In real life, this is the aspect called faith. But people don't realize that faith simply means allowing the law of the universe to fulfill itself through the seeds you have sown. This is scientific faith.

LAW #7: PERSISTENCE

When you sow corn, you wait for it to mature in its due season. You do not get restless and uproot it and plant beans or something else. Do you? When you set an objective in life and start a project to achieve it, you have to persist till you achieve it. Changing your mind every day and chasing something new every day without having achieved the previous one is the perfect recipe for failure. Learn to pray without ceasing, till you get what you have asked for.

LAW #8: PASSION

While the crop is growing you visit it regularly to weed the grass, munch the soil, and keep animals away, and sometimes add fertilizer. In life, you must protect your dreams from the birds of people's negative thinking and discouragement, you must weed off any people in your life that are trying to run you down rather than build you up. You must keep feeding your mind and building your faith with inspiration. You must be a life-long learner who is always improving and becoming more fertile. You must surround yourself with people who have done what you are doing so that their energy and guidance can serve as manure for your dream. Your passion is your fuel. Only those who are in love with their dream see their dream come true.

LAW #9: NETWORKING

Sometimes you team up with other people to form a farming *njangui*. The whole team lands on your farm and brings down the whole hill in one day. The following day they move to the other person's farm. Every member of the group is a specialist at something. Because of the massive action and division of labor, work is lighter and enjoyable, and everyone ends up with more work done than they could possibly have done alone.

This is the power of the mastermind alliance. You need to build your personal success network using people whose hearts and minds resonate with yours. This is what Jesus meant when he said that "when two or three are gathered in my name I am in their midst". Psychology has proven that when two or more minds are focused on a single objective, there is a resultant mind that is more powerful than the sum of its parts.

LAW #10: RECEIVING

When it is harvesting time, you do not ask for anyone's permission or approval in order to enjoy the fruits of your labor. You do not beg God for a miracle or doubt if you deserve the fruits. No, all that nature has poured out as harvest through your farm, is automatically yours. When you are harvesting the fruits of your labor, do not apologize to those who envy you or claim you had some advantages that they don't.

You do not feel guilty that you have a rich harvest and some people don't. No, you reap with joy and you don't leave some food behind. When success comes to you it comes in a measure that can be overwhelming and cause you to wonder if you actually deserve it. Remember that it is not a random blessing but the fulfillment of the law. It is the seeds you cultivated that have multiplied. It is not a miracle, it is perfectly natural.

There are people who will say you are successful because you have joined a cult, or because you come from a rich home, or because you are well connected. Some of your friends will try to make you feel guilty for being so successful while they are not. Nonsense! Enjoy your success. The only thing they can do to help themselves is to let your example inspire them. If they fail to do so, it is not your fault.

LAW #11: MULTIPLICATION

The first thing you do with any harvest is that you select the very best crop and save it as seed for the next season. No matter what form of success you enjoy, always save the best as a seed to your greater success. For example, open a bank account into which you save 10% of every money that enters your hand and make sure you never withdraw from it.

The day will come when you will need capital for your next project, then you will repeat the cycle. This is what the law of tithing is really about. Harvest the first tenth of every gift you receive and save it as seed. A tenth of your time, your energy, your money, your relationships, your talent, everything, should be invested into the creation of the better version of your tomorrow.

LAW #12: GIVING

As you enjoy your harvest, you find that it tastes sweeter when shared. The power of sharing, the meaning of community or communion. Sharing your good fortune with others and bringing joy to their lives is the ultimate success. No matter how many hours we spend each day in worship and adoration, sharing with others is the most powerful form of worship, for it testifies in a tangible way that we recognize the presence of God in others. No matter how thankful we say we are, giving is the only tangible proof that we are grateful to our Source because by giving, we become the source to others.

***

Here I have given you a resume of the Twelve Fundamental Laws of Success. No matter which book you read, which seminar you attend, which courses you take, which movies you watch on the subject of life, everything they teach you will always boil down to these twelve laws. On very rare occasions will you find them articulated in the comprehensive manner in which we have done them here. Yes, by returning to the lowliest of places (our mothers' farms), we have unveiled a model of life that beats all the knowledge of the world.

This wisdom has been lying fallow within you because you have not been aware that it was there. You were busy chasing for knowledge in the amphitheaters and seeking success secrets in books. Now that I have caused you to remember what you know, wake up now and put it to use to transform your life and your world.

7

Chapter 7: Lead the Change

Leading change is about becoming so resilient that you go beyond your personal survival and start helping other people to navigate change. When you focus on helping other people solve their problems, solutions to your own problems have a miraculous way of showing up. It is not magic anyway. It is logical. Focusing on other people distracts you from fear, regret, worry, and panic. It gives you expanded awareness and unleashes your genius. The reason why your own solutions appear miraculous is that they are effortless. The reason why they are effortless is that you have become bigger than your problems.

Focusing on other people gives you a bigger head and a bigger heart. But make no mistake; you cannot give what you do not have. Focusing on other people does not mean escaping from your own challenges. In order to lead others, you must first lead yourself. Here is how to prepare yourself to be there for other people:

Take stock of the intrinsic strengths, talents, and gifts that make you unique. Because you are a unique presence on this planet, you can become irreplaceable if you master how to infuse your work with your uniqueness.

Take stock of the Opportunities that your strengths, talents, and gifts create for you. Ask yourself how you can leverage these opportunities. Keep a journal in which you jot down all the creative ideas that come to your mind. In life, we often see what we are looking for. If you train yourself to be an opportunity hunter, you will always see opportunity.

Take stock of the Challenges (weaknesses, threats, and risks) that are facing you and any venture you are planning. Knowing your vulnerabilities is the best defense. If you have a plan for managing and compensating for them, no person or external circumstance will surprise you by taking advantage of them.

Take stock of the Specialized Knowledge you possess and what new knowledge you need to acquire in order to be able to perform at your best. The golden rule of survival in the information economy is life-long learning. Life-long learning is self-directed. Learn to find out what you need to learn, how to learn it, when to learn it, and what to do with what you learn.

Take stock of the Stakeholders that you are accountable to or that you need to work with or work for. Who do you need to have therapeutic conversations with? Who do you need to brainstorm with? Who do you need to include in your team? Who do you need to serve?

Help others solve their problems, and yours will take care of themselves.

In my daily posts within the Godfrey Esoh Network, I usually share real-life stories of people whose transformation I have been part of. I recently published a story about a lady KS and her daughter DT who are amazing embodiments of resilience. Someone read the story of KS and DT and was so moved that he sent me a donation of $100 for mom and daughter. He insisted on keeping his act of love anonymous, so as the hearts of KS and DT are swelling with gratitude, they do not know what their angel looks like.

That same week, my friend Godlove Njisong asked me to resurrect the Esoh Angel Network so that we could galvanize support for the teenage inventor in Bamenda who has built his own toy plane from scratch and succeeded to make it fly, although he is not going to school and his father is blind. These two incidents occurred while I was putting this book together, so I took it as an invitation to use the Esoh Angel Network as a fitting case study for this chapter on Leading the Change.

According to Dale's Cone of Experience (1969) as adapted by Heidi Milia Anderson, Ph.D., at the University of Kentucky, people generally remember:

- 10% of what they Read,
- 20% of what they Hear,
- 30% of what they See,
- 50% of what they See and Hear,
- 70% of what they Say and Write, and
- 90% of what they Do as they perform a task.

My unique experience as an author and coach is fueled by the fact that I am first and foremost a scientist and educator. In my continuing quest to help people internalize and materialize my messages, I came up with a strange idea in 2018. It occurred to me that I had built a huge network of adorable people that were being inspired on a daily basis by my transformative messages. It dawned on me that when people are PASSIVE OBSERVERS, they gain nothing, but when they are ACTIVE PARTICIPANTS, they get transformed. So, I started the Esoh Angel Network as an initiative that transforms my SOCIAL NETWORK into an IMPACT NETWORK.

The Esoh Angel Network initiative gives members of my network the opportunity to put into practice the inspirational messages they receive from me daily. I am of the conviction that no matter how good a church sermon or a motivational message is, anyone who does not DO SOMETHING about it does not really believe it, no matter what they say with their lips.

When we just started the Esoh Angel Network, we encouraged people to do monthly free-will donations of 5000FCFA. At the end of each month, we would pool the donations together, randomly select someone in need, and surprise that person with a miracle. Members donate only when they are able and willing. There is no obligation on anyone.

These past two years have been incredible. More than 100 Angels have donated to our initiative, enabling us to put smiles on the faces of hundreds of people.

We have supplied breakfast and sanitation items to 40 handicapped children in a rehabilitation center.

We have paid for emergency surgery for a desperate case in the hospital and saved a life.

We have provided food and school needs to over 50 children in two orphanages.

We have paid for CD4 Count tests for 20 people living with HIV as a means of supporting their effective management.

We have educated and helped young women to get screened for cervical cancer.

We have paid for echography for 12 pregnant women who could otherwise not afford it.

We have bought protective and work gear for a youth who makes his living by scavenging dumpsites to collect electronic parts, refurbish, and sell.

We have helped an internally displaced mother who does not know where her husband is, to start a small business to feed her children.

Although this objective data looks compelling enough, our goal is not really to "dump" aid on people the way charity foundations normally do. First of all, we do not receive grants from any institutional donors. We inspire members of our network to put their love in practice by being one another's keeper.

Secondly, we do not pay attention to the amount of aid we provide. We rather focus on using these little tokens as a means of reminding people that they are not alone, lifting their spirits through unconditional love, and cheering them on to heal and elevate themselves toward their divine destiny.

The people who give, do not give because they have; they give because they believe in the power of sharing and the law of compensation that never fails to multiply the harvest of those who sow on fertile ground. This is the FAITH FACTOR.

The people who receive do not receive because they asked for it. Most of the time, we do not know them and they do not know us. Our community volunteers select them at random based on their observed needs. When we surprise them with a miracle of kindness, we are certain that we have rejuvenated their spirits. This is the HOPE FACTOR.

What binds the givers and the receivers together is the inspired community that keeps growing around my message of our divine identity, our unlimited potential, and our glorious destiny as the unique manifestations of One Eternal Source. This is the LOVE FACTOR.

When you put faith, hope, and love together, you have our purpose, which is encapsulated in Saint Paul's celebrated treatise on Love in Chapter 13 of his first letter to the Corinthians.

I have had many struggles since the Esoh Angel Network project started. Who am I to be a philanthropist in a world where the word "Philanthropy" is normally associated with the likes of Bill Clinton, Bill Gates, Oprah Winfrey, Akon, Mo Ibrahim, and Tony Elumelu? What do I have? Well, it is all about "disruption".

The conventional model of philanthropy is that people build fame and fortune, then leverage these two to create impact. Naturally, one would ask whether those who become philanthropists following this model do so out of the goodness of their hearts, or because it is expedient to spend their money on charity than on taxes. Without watering down the merit of these great people, I believe that it takes more courage to cultivate the spirit of sharing when you are a nobody who has nothing. That way, you are forced to make an offering of the one thing you do have - yourself.

Thus, I am a strong advocate for the alternative model of philanthropy. This alternative model inspires people to think in terms of "us" rather than "me", to build communities rather than self, and to graft selflessness into their character right from the beginning. This is why I empower people to expand their awareness beyond their personal survival needs. I lead them to practice the principles of success by making it natural to "be the source of abundance" for other people. In a generation of social media madness, I endeavor to transform my social network into an impact network. The whole satisfaction comes from having created something new that has the power to change the world.

Communities are powerful enough to take care of one another when they come together in the spirit of selfless love. The dependency spirit, the charity mentality, and the "foreign aid syndrome" are moral cancers that have eaten into the spirits of Africans and damaged their sense of pride and their potential for greatness. The

Godfrey Esoh Network is one little step in the direction of disrupting this social ill and empowering people to build and sustain community wealth.

2

Part 2: Story of a Resilient Soul

"I am not what happened to me…I am what I choose to become."
~Carl Gustav Jung~

8

Chapter 8: Rags to Riches

I was born as the 8th child among 10 siblings in a small village called Mbatu, in Bamenda, Cameroon. My mother had no education or employment. She worked on the farms on weekdays to provide the food we needed and sold in the market on Saturdays to generate the extra cash she needed to take care of our education, healthcare, and other needs. Shortly before I was born, my father had retired back home from Nigeria where he had worked as a steward for the British colonial administrators.

Apart from the items that the Land Rover had transported together with my family from Lagos to Bamenda, my father had no property, no business, no investments, and no retirement savings. Even the house in which I was born was not ours. It belonged to my father's uncle who was heir to my great-grandfather. Making my entry into this world through a large village family headed by an uneducated mom and a retired dad living in a borrowed house in a remote village in a developing country was quite the recipe for a life of struggle. And yes, my childhood was full of the kind of struggle that would appear unimaginable not only to those born under better circumstances but even to the younger generation of people that were born two decades later in the same environment.

The other day I had a very long conversation with Glory, a lady whom I grew up knowing as a family friend, and who turned out to be a "mother" to me while I was in the university. Glory is in Texas, and I am in Boston, and if you understand how America is, you will forgive people for spending six months without talking to each other. So when we "caught" each other at a good time last week, that call turned out to be like a Pontifical High Mass.

Glory is the kind of soulful person who knows how to penetrate your soul because her own life has never been an easy one. I dare say she is a pure soul because she is one of the very few human beings I know who live straight from the heart. At one point in our conversation, she expressed her amazement at the messages I write every day and how they are touching lives, and then she asked me how on earth I can manage to remember some of the things I narrate in my stories.

Without realizing it, I blurted out incidents from my childhood, some so old that a normal human being would need to undergo hypnotherapy before remembering them. And since that conversation, my spirit has been rattled because it is like a floodgate got opened.

I remember how at the age of about 4, we were living in Pa Tamu's house, the successor of my father's grandfather whom I mentioned earlier. What was peculiar about this house was that it was one of those ancient houses that were built of sticks and mud, and then cemented. From every indication, Pa Tamu was a rich man in his day. The proof is that he had this house in the village, while he lived in another one at Old Town Bamenda.

I remember my childhood in that house so well because it was a linear structure with a living room in the middle and two bedrooms on both sides. By the time I became self-conscious, my kid sisters (the twins) had been born, and so I was sharing the other room with the rest of my siblings. The bigger boys were sleeping on a bamboo bed in the firewood kitchen. Due to overcrowding in our house and very little room to play, I once fell into a basin of hot water that our mom had prepared to dilute and bathe the twins with. The last traces of those burn scars disappeared from my laps when I was already a teenager.

I remember that our backyard was made up of lush green bushes with wild vegetables and fruit trees, separating us from the compound of Ta Zagh-Teku and Pa Asanga (a.k.a Mbatucam). Under one of the palm trees was an open pit-toilet whose flooring was made up of sticks that were apparently older than me. Because of the clear and present danger of falling into the pit, easing one's self every morning was thus a meditative experience, and maybe that is how I started learning the power of attention, focus, and concentration.

There were some palm trees that were not so tall, but they had started bearing fruit. At the age of 5, I was already climbing trees. I have a scar on my right arm, just below my inner elbow, that looks as sharp and clean as an incision mark from a surgical knife. I got that mark the first day I fell from a palm tree and the sharp needles of a palm branch caught my arm. It is pointless to mention the number of times I subsequently fell from guava trees, mango trees, etc., and passed out for some seconds before regaining consciousness. In our childhood, when you fell from a tree, you were flogged. So if you were not visibly bleeding, you were better off hiding it.

It is around this same age of 5 that we used to go to the Asanga's on Sunday afternoons to watch "Tam-Tam Weekend" on Cameroon Television. The veranda was always so clean that we would take off our shoes before climbing it and then cling on the window protector to watch the small Black and White TV screen through the window. It is the Asanga kids that made me realize that the children of rich people were normal people because they were quite fond of us and would play with us until someone from either family came to chase us home. Till today, Franklin is still the best goal-keeper Mbatu has ever had.

There was this rich neighbor living in a really modern house, with cars, and everything that made you realize that there was something different about your own family. He had a tap at the back of his kitchen from which I used to fetch water every morning. Apart from fetching water, I had another morning ritual. I would open the tap to drip very slowly so that my bucket or gallon would not fill up fast. And what did I need the extra time for? To hang around and sniff the aroma from the kitchen in which the cook was preparing breakfast for Papa – usually fried egg and potatoes or ripe plantains. I was between 5 and 6, but that aroma has never left me.

Next door to the firewood kitchen in which my older brothers were sleeping was another room that served as both a living room and kitchen for my uncle Pa Matty. Oh, there is not a single angelic soul that I have seen on this earth like Pa Matty. All the children who grew up in the Tamu's compound have stories about Pa Matty and his cooking. Since he was living alone, all the women in the compound used to send him food.

No matter how many varieties of meals he found on his kitchen bamboo table, he would pour everything inside a pot and porridge it together (the only exception being *achu*). But the *achu soup*, bitter leaf soup, okro, corn-chaff, fufu corn, etc., would all go into the same pot. Well, Pa Matty never used to lock his door, so we would help ourselves to his cocktail whenever we had a chance to sneak in and out without getting caught.

I remember the first time in my life when I became aware of feelings, emotion, love, or whatever you want to call it. My mother was brought home by her brother Pa Martin Wabara with a sprained ankle. She had slipped on a rotten cocoyam leaf by a spring in the farm at Atugh-Ndagh. Fortunately, another woman had found her and gone for help. When I watched her limping and being supported into the house, it dawned on me for the first time that the pain she was feeling was because she had gone out to look for food for us. I was 4 years old then, but I remember it like yesterday.

It is during those days that mom could not go to the farm that Pa Matty formally invited us to eat in his house. Unfortunately, the memory of the food I ate in Pa Matty's house after school one afternoon was porridge corn with no beans. Not that I did not appreciate it. But there is no way I can ever listen to the "cornmeal porridge" line in Bob Marley's "No woman no cry", without this childhood incident coming back to me.

My dad had a special liking for me because, since the return of my family from Nigeria, he and my mom had had two girls before me, and then the birth after me had turned out to be a set of twin girls. I was 3 years old when my kid sisters were born. If you recall the sensation that twins used to create in those days, you will imagine how crowded our house used to be. Dad used to go out for a drink in the evenings, and at one point, since he could not get rid of me, he started taking me along.

I remember the sensation I created at home when I came back and announced in broken Mbatu language *"Begh baba ghe toh nooh ndo'o"* (Papa and I went to the store and drink wine). The "ndo'o" (wine) that I had tasted for my first time was actually "Fanta", and of course, the gas in it had gotten me "drunk".

The famous off-license at Njimafor at the time was owned by Pa Tita Atanga, which my infant tongue could only pronounce as "Pa Titangs". As I said, I was just above 3 and not yet speaking fluently. But in case you ever hear of a TT Junction at Njimafor, know that it is Tita Atanga's Junction that they are talking about. That is where the Njimafor Veteran's Club used to hold until the Anglophone Crisis that broke out a few years ago.

The year I was born, Dad was a licensed palm oil wholesale distributor for Lobe Palm Estate. I hear that my "born-house" was a lavish one and that this palm oil business was the reason why I was nicknamed *"nkap mevere"* (oil money). But by the time I was 5 years old, I was keen enough to notice that the oil drums that were being offloaded in our yard no longer carried my dad's initials. A takeover had occurred, and it would take me 30 years to know the truth about what really happened.

But being a resilient "Lagos Boy" who loved work and celebration, dad used to go to Nah-kah in neighboring Bali and fetch sugarcane, only to come and share at Njimafor. When he was ascending the hill from Pa Nkarimbi and approaching Pa Tita Atanga's Off Licence, he would start singing his mantra, "Papa I trowey...Papa I troweyyy", and behold, he would dump the bunch of sugarcane at the entrance of the bar, go and grab his beer, and everyone who wanted to eat sugarcane would pass and drag his cane. Whoever was honest or appreciative enough to go into the bar and give him money, he would collect and say, "thank you". I was a keen observer of all this because since he had taken me to "TT Junction" at the age of 3, the bushes around that area had become my favorite spot for fetching fruits and chasing birds, just so that I could spy on the bar for when my dad would show up.

I was precisely seven years old when we built our own family house and moved in. Pa Mundi-Ngu, Pa Zancho, and Pa Jacob were the master builders of Mbatu in those days. With my little gallon, I dashed to the stream like a rabbit to fetch water and fill the drums that were never getting full. With my tiny feet like the play-sticks of a xylophone, I joyfully pounded the mud with which they made sun-dried bricks to build our house.

As soon as our house had a roof over it, we moved in. Some of the windows were covered with plastic bags. There were no ceilings;

there was no floor; the walls were not plastered; and there was no electricity.

The last memory I have of my mother's father Tata Barnabas Fru Awasum was when he visited us in our new house. I still recall his bicycle leaning on the palm tree that still stands at the entrance to our compound to this day. A few months later, my cousin, Ngia Eli Magha, and her husband came to break the news to my mother that Tata Bana was no more. And that was my first experience of watching women wail, weep and roll on the ground. In those days, deaths were rare and far between.

One night, another unexpected tragedy struck. On his way back from Bamenda Modern Bakery (Nangah Bakery) where he used to work, my dad was carrying a bunch of used aluminum sheets that he had been buying and saving to roof our outdoor firewood kitchen. A speeding car hit him from behind and dragged him from the Hospital Roundabout to below the Regional Hospital maternity. For some miraculous reason, he did not die, but he would stay bedridden for almost two years. Being the youngest son, I had my induction into caregiving at the age of 8.

When he started recovering and could use his crutches to go out of the house, he opened a provision store. And guess who became the assistant shop-keeper? Me! At the age of 9. Yes, at the age of 9, I was selling in a provision store and lighting cigarettes for all the smokers in Njimafor. God alone knows why I don't smoke, but I was the kind of kid who could tell what brand of cigarette someone was smoking from a distance.

It was while I was taking care of our little shop one morning that the news came that the whole of Mbatu village was swinging to an automatic public holiday mode. Our Fon (tribal king) had *"gone missing"* and tradition demanded that no one could farm, hunt, or celebrate anything in the village unless the Fon was *"found again"*. And so, at the age of 9, my curiosity about African Tradition and

Spirituality began. This was to be followed by my fascination with the work of Baba Nkemtsab, the Master Seer and Healer of our land, who turned out to be my maternal granduncle, and whom I eventually got close to because of frequent family visits.

I never used to be a bright student in school. I would always stay in my mother's kitchen and wait for the last bell before I rush off to school, often with some cassava or sweet potatoes in my hand. I have a vivid memory of how my sister Therese used to come and peep through the window and wave at me just to make sure I was doing fine. Ah, now that I think of it, T used to be a beautiful, adorable, and loving angel of a sister.

Marie grew up with my grandmom, Mama Bertha Adey, at Atugh-Mambang, and attended Catholic School Munjuh-Mbatu. In those early primary school days, I used to see her only during school competitions. When it came to football and Choral Music, Njimafor had no match. When it came to traditional dance and handball, Munjuh had no match. And my sister, Mary Yaya as they used to call her, was a star.

In those glory days, Pa Fonmedig Anthony was HeadMaster of Catholic School Munjuh, and Mr. Chin Francis was Choir Master of the Whistling Birds of Njimafor. Those were the days when Munjuh girls used to weave and wear "ngwashi" (fibre skirts), and boys like Zophini would play the drum until you would hear it "talk".

Some years ago I stumbled on my primary school report card and was bemused to find that in Class 1 at Catholic School Njimafor, I was number 23 in a class of about 52. There was a slight improvement in Class 2. But then in Class 3, a miracle came out of nowhere.

I came in 3rd position, and for some strange reason, it was in this year that a prize award ceremony was organized in our school. Receiving a prize for academic performance changed my life. It was clear to me that the bucket and books I received were worth several bags of vegetables that my mom would have sold in Bamenda Market, after a whole season of labor.

So, believe it or not, it is at the age of 8 that I had my first light bulb moment; I discovered that by cultivating my brain and putting it to good use, I could earn the same things that would otherwise be earned through intensive labor and time. I was not born a genius – I only decided to be one, when I stumbled on the idea that my brain was my passport out of poverty.

These then are the first nine years of my life, just as you would expect from a good Catholic boy who prays his Novenas. Before you ask me where such vivid memories come from, please remember that this reflection started with Glory's soulful probing. What I have come to realize is that all our memories are with us. We just need the right keys to access them. And the benefit of accessing our memories is that it gives us the opportunity to connect the dots and find the pattern that gives our life meaning and helps us define our purpose. Each time I say you should turn your scars into stars, remember that you cannot do so if you do not remember the scars in the first place.

Most of us lock up the memories of our past because we are afraid of facing the pain. But the more you come to terms with who you are, where you come from, and where you are going, you will be amazed to realize that you have more to be thankful for than you have to complain about; you have more to be joyful for than you have to regret about, and you have more to be hopeful for than you have to be afraid of.

It is my understanding that most people have little or no memory of the first eight years of their lives, which paradoxically, turns out to be the period when the personality is formed through family nurturing and social conditioning. The whole premise of the clinical use of hypnotherapy is that if you can relive a certain hidden experience, it will give you the power to rediscover yourself, heal certain wounds, or understand certain patterns that you can leverage to master your present and engineer your future. The only other time that some people access their subconscious minds, see their entire life as a movie, and emerge as gods, is when they have near-death experiences.

But if you practice soulful living and reflective thinking like I do and teach, I bet you that you will never need hypnotherapy or a near-death experience before embracing your true power.

How would your life change if you got to the place where you fear nothing, worry about nothing, and dare anything? How would your life change if you got to the place where you know that love is all that matters? The lessons I am sharing with you come from a deeply personal place. They are not philosophical speculations or data points drawn from experimentation.

I did not learn resilience in the mechanical or academic way that most people do. As you can see from the reflection I have just shared, Resilience is what and who I have been, right from the start. Through this book, it is a piece of myself that I share with you in love and with the hope that you will make the most of it to transform your life the way I keep transforming mine.

Chapter 9: Ugly War, Broken Dreams

At the age of 35, I was at the peak of my career. I had fought my way through hardship upon hardship and braved it from failure to failure to attain what anyone would consider the summit. I was the Rector and President of a higher education institute called Jomatt Polytechnic Batibo. Here is the story of how my career as a higher education manager evolved, and how it was brought to a crashing halt by the armed conflict that broke out as a result of the Cameroon Anglophone crisis.

I was 26 years old when I joined the Institute of Applied Medical Sciences (IAMS) Buea as an instructor in April 2007. In August 2007, the deputy director in charge of teaching took a study leave and traveled to the United States where she had picked up a Ph.D. scholarship. The Head of Department for Medical Laboratory Science was promoted to Deputy Director in charge of Teaching, and I was appointed the new Head of Department for Medical Laboratory Science. Through another interesting unfolding of circumstances, I was promoted to Deputy Director in charge of Teaching within three months.

Before my arrival at IAMS, the institute had won a grant from the England-Africa Partnerships in Higher Education (EAP) Initiative, sponsored by the British Council. This grant worth 60,000 British Pounds involved a collaboration between the Institute of Applied Medical Sciences, the Department of Nursing of the University of Buea, and the School of Nursing and Midwifery of the University of East Anglia in the United Kingdom, to reinforce the capacity for degree-level nursing education in Cameroon.

The project team from England visited in September 2007 and the project was launched through a national nursing conference hosted by the University of Buea. Because of my role as deputy director in charge of teaching at IAMS, I was instrumental in organizing the conference and coordinating it to a successful end. After the conference, the project team from the three institutions relocated to IAMS where they held project meetings to design the Masters in Nursing Education program and the undergraduate nursing curriculum that had resulted from the conference.

Here again, although I was not a nurse, my presence became crucial as my computer and office skills were needed to take minutes, process all paperwork that was needed during the working sessions, and prepare project reports. My inputs into the project became so significant that by the end of the visit of that week, the project team was unanimous on the idea that I should be the IAMS staff representative on the Cameroon project team that would be going for a return project visit to England the six weeks later. This was a role originally reserved for the Head of Department for Nursing, but clearly, my project management expertise was judged to be more beneficial to the future of the project.

I was humbled when the unexpected change was announced and

frankly, it would have been weird to have the Head of Department for medical laboratory science on a nursing project team while the Head of Department for nursing stayed behind. The good fortune here was that, as I have hinted earlier, by this time I was no longer the Head of Department for medical laboratory science. Barely one month into her promotion, the deputy director in charge of teaching got recruited into the public service and resigned from IAMS thereby creating a vacancy in that office. Since we were planning for the start of a new academic year, I was commissioned to take charge of the academic planning for that year.

This exercise caused me to revisit the whole system through which the institute recruited staff, assigned courses, managed the teaching and learning process, and paid staff. I was reviewing the system with the intention of "mastering" it so that I could do the work I had been assigned to do. But along the line, I got creative. I drafted a new model for academic and staff planning that was shockingly going to result in the institute saving close to 50% of the annual budget it had spent on teaching for the previous years. I instinctively knew that this money part would catch the president's attention, so I tossed the plan to him during one of our morning management briefings. His response was simple, if I could develop my new model in detail and give him a complete implementation plan, he would empower me to implement it.

That is how I stumbled into my new appointment as deputy director in charge of teaching, barely a few days before the launching of the nursing project. So, by the time the project team was being reconstituted, my designation was deputy director in charge of teaching. Not only was I very handy to the project team in terms of project management skills, but I was also now higher in rank than the Head of Department for nursing. Her displacement appeared logical and thankfully did not spark up any conflict.

The project was initially conceived as a means by which the expertise of the School of Nursing and Midwifery of the University of East Anglia would be harnessed to train nurse teachers for the Cameroon partners, that is, the Institute of Applied Medical Sciences Buea and the department of nursing of the University of Buea. The problem addressed by this project was monumental.

Since the colonial days, 90% of healthcare in Cameroon had been in the hands of State Registered Nurses. The State Registered Nurse was the highest rank that a nurse could attain in Cameroon until the late 1990s. SRNs were trained in professional schools run by the Ministry of Public Health and posted to run health centers and hospital wards. The doctor: patient ratio in Cameroon is still about 1:10,000. As an example, my local Mbachongwa health area that covers the villages of Mbatu, Nsongwa, and Chomba, is still being served by one health center that is headed by a nurse. In order to see a doctor, patients from this area must travel to the Regional hospital in Bamenda town.

In 1997 the Faculty of Health Sciences of the University of Buea launched the first bachelor's degree program in Nursing in Cameroon. The aim of the program was to complement the course content of the SRN program with the scientific prowess and managerial skills that would result in a higher grade of nurses more capable of undertaking the task bestowed upon them as champions of healthcare in Cameroon.

In the year 2000, as a result of the Higher Education reforms, private higher education institutions emerged in Cameroon as a response to the huge pressure that the high demand for higher education was having on the few, often underequipped state universities. The government conceived the private higher education sector to serve as a professionalization arm of the higher education sector. After high school, students could enroll in a private higher institute and complete a higher national diploma in a professional discipline in two or three years. As such higher institutes began emerging, the nursing profession also benefited.

So, by 2007 there were three undergraduate nursing certificates recognized in Cameroon: The Bachelor's degree of the University of Buea and other private universities that had emerged, the Higher National Diploma of the Ministry of Higher education awarded to graduates of approved private higher institutes, and the traditional State Registered Nurse diploma awarded by the Ministry of Health to graduates of the public nursing training institutions.

The major challenge faced by this evolution in Cameroonian nursing education was the problem of lack of teachers. While the State Registered Nursing schools depended on SRNs who had obtained a teaching certificate, and the private nursing schools depended on Bachelor's degree nurses from the University of Buea, the University of Buea itself did not have the graduate level nurses to teach on its degree program.

Also, the higher education regulations permitted a top-up degree program for diploma holders but this could be implemented only if there were sufficient teaching staff with at least a master's degree. It is against this backdrop that the England Africa Partnership project was designed to develop a standardized undergraduate nursing curriculum that could be implemented by all the nursing schools, and strain master's degree holders who would teach these degree programs.

I still remember the look on the face of the gentleman who interviewed me when we went for a visa application at the British High Commission in Yaoundé. I was the babyface among the delegation of four that included the two nursing lecturers from the University of Buea, the President of IAMS (my boss), and myself.

When the guy asked me, "so what is your specific role on this visit?" I wonder what he was expecting as a response, but I know he didn't see this coming; "I will be teaching the nursing lecturers at our partner University in England how to package their course material and deploy it online for use by the master's students who will be taking part of their course in Cameroon." Of course, I got the visa.

Meeting the Vice-Chancellor of the University of East Anglia was one of the most illuminating experiences I had had till then. He came five minutes late for our meeting and apologized that he had just flown in that morning from Hong-Kong and had lost track of time. I asked my boss whether a Cameroonian Vice-Chancellor ever apologized for being late even by one hour. The guy was a Cambridge graduate and the minister of education was his classmate. He was the type of influential person who would sit in their offices and receive a delegation from organizations like the Gates Foundation seeking projects to fund.

His vote of confidence served as a pillar to the success of our project, and for me personally, the few insights I picked by reading between the lines as we interacted with this great man, went a long way in boosting my confidence and shaping my outlook on life. The photo I took with him still makes me laugh till today; the contrast in height, age, color, and my oversized suit.

If you have watched the Nigerian movie "Usophia in London" starring Nkem Owo a.k.a Ukwa, then you can figure out how my first few days in the UK would have looked like had my boss not "had me on a leash" most of the time. We missed the train a few times before I figured that trains worked on schedules. I had reared rabbits in my childhood and seeing so many of them strolling around took me off guard. I almost caught one before my boss warned me against it.

During the official dinner offered by our host, I asked for my turkey to be "well-cooked" only to find that I couldn't eat it because the British "well-cooked" meat is the Cameroonian version of "par-boiled". While hanging out in the campus pub I decided to taste some foreign beer only to regret it. It cost lots of money but tasted like water compared to Cameroonian beer. On the night before our departure, I sneaked out of the guest house into the campus club where a Jamaican reggae band was having a concert and you could hardly see who you were dancing with because almost everyone was smoking weed.

When we returned from our trip to East Anglia, the next phase of the project was for the Vice-Chancellor of the University of Buea to officially launch the special scholarship program under which twelve nurses were to be recruited for the first batch of the Master of Nursing Education program. I worked through the Christmas break of that year coordinating activities between Buea and East Anglia. The selection list came out in December and the students formally started school in January.

In April this cohort of 12 master's students was to travel to the UK for one intensive month of study at the School of Nursing and Midwifery. This was part of their blended-learning two-year program. I was again assigned to process the paperwork for these 12 nurses, accompany them to England, and bring them back. Fortunately for me, the people that had earned that scholarship were all great people. Apart from administrative and project correspondences that kept me busy in England, I had little or no babysitting to do. By the time we came back, I had had twelve new great friends who were the future of nursing in Cameroon.

The collateral benefit from this project was that it dawned on me that I was a Bachelor's degree holder managing a project that was helping other people earn a Master's degree. I had enough common sense to know that if I stayed on the same spot, some of these people would eventually become my bosses. It is that year that I enrolled for my own Master's program, which I completed in 2010.

Thanks to the official recognition by the Ministry of Higher Education, the Institute of Applied Medical Sciences was formally transformed into the Higher Institute of Applied Medical Sciences in May 2008. I spent the summer of 2008 elaborating the total quality management manual for this new higher education institution and started implementing it during the 2008-2009 academic year.

As a means of giving me the free reign to implement this management plan, my role was switched again from deputy director in charge of teaching to deputy director in charge of administration. I was now the administrative director of the Higher Institute of Applied Medical Sciences, second in rank only to the Executive President and Founder. In Cameroonian higher education, I was the youngest to occupy that rank at the time.

After a three-year break from education, working as a laboratory scientist with the Ministry of Public Health, I enrolled for Ph.D. at the University of Calabar in Nigeria. Unfortunately, my arrival in Calabar coincided with the year that Nigeria has had its longest university lecturers' strike in recent times.

I eventually abandoned and came back to Cameroon and took a teaching position at the National Polytechnic Bamenda (NPB), as a means of passing the time while waiting for the strike to be called off. Two days after my recruitment I was surprised with an appointment as Coordinator of Degree Programs in the School of Medical and Biomedical Sciences.

My job was to coordinate the academic planning, teaching, learning, and assessment for the top-up bachelor's degree programs in nursing and medical laboratory science, under the mentorship of the University of Buea. After one year in this position, I was promoted to Dean of the School of Medical and Biomedical Sciences, a position that made me directly responsible for the Higher National Diploma program in Nursing, the State Registered Nursing Program, The Bachelor of Technology program in Nursing, the Higher National Diploma program in Medical Laboratory Science, and the Bachelor of Technology program in Medical Laboratory Science. Work at NPB became so engaging that I forgot about the Ph.D. program in Calabar altogether.

The office of Dean of the School of Medical and Biomedical Sciences was certainly lower in rank than that of Administrative Director which I had held at the Higher Institute of Applied Medical Sciences. However, it was not rank that I was looking for, at least, not yet. National Polytechnic Bamenda was the oldest, largest, and most popular private university institution in English-speaking Cameroon, and becoming a top-ranking staff there certainly scored some extra points on my career profile. Even as Dean, one earned a lot of respect on a greater scale than the Deputy Director of a smaller institution.

But the respect came with a price. The School of Medical and Biomedical Sciences that I was heading was six times larger in population than the entire Higher Institute of Applied Medical Sciences where I used to be Deputy Director. The students of National Polytechnic Bamenda had one of the worst reputations in Bamenda in terms of conduct and professionalism. And on campus, out of the ten professional schools that made up the polytechnic, the School of Medical and Biomedical Sciences was second only to the School of Engineering when it came to indiscipline.

You would expect health science students to be the best-behaved and most focused students in any environment, but in those days, that was not the case. Most people went to medical school not because they had a vocation to serve fellow humans but because a health science certificate was perceived as a ticket for easy employment at home, or a password to easy money for those who would succeed to travel abroad. And of course, traveling abroad was every student's after-school dream.

I mustered the audacity to reform the School of Medical and Biomedical Sciences. The changes in number and quality of staff, dresscode, student conduct, class attendance, follow-up of teaching, and quality of assessment, just to name a few, were so sweeping that within a year "Esoh" had become a household name on campus. That is also when I learned that the easiest way to become a star is to get students to hate you.

But it is not only students that had trouble with the changes that the school was undergoing in my presence. I expected that. The unexpected part was the number of enemies I made among the old staff and my bosses in the central administration whose normal way of doing business was being disrupted by the quality standards I was introducing in the school of Medical and Biomedical Sciences. As an innovative, progressive, young, and energetic medical educationist who was more passionate about the quality of graduates I sent out than about how much I pleased my colleagues and bosses or was liked by my students, surviving in that environment for three years was quite a miracle.

Shortly after my appointment as Dean in September 2014, I was sent to Germany as part of a delegation whose mission was to develop a blueprint for a mentorship agreement between the School of Medical and Biomedical Sciences, and Charité Medical University in Berlin, the 300 year old most famous medical university in Europe. We had three days of intensive work with the international collaboration office and the professors who had been designated to head the collaboration project whose goals included helping National Polytechnic Bamenda to design, build, and run a school of medicine, with the approval of the Ministry of Higher Education in Cameroon.

The following summer, the German project team paid a return visit to Cameroon for a one week working session with a team we had constituted from the NPB top management and some professors from the Faculty of Health Sciences of the University of Bamenda. Land for the construction of the medical school had been bought before I ever came to NPB. During my service as dean, we completed the curriculum work, and drafted a pathway for securing equipment, staff, and other requirements that would be needed on the ground to qualify the envisaged school of medicine for approval by the Ministry of Higher Education.

I also nursed an innovative approach to graduate training. The management of NPB was concerned about the fact that an increasing number of higher education institutions were being approved by the government and their presence, coupled with that of the newly created University of Bamenda, was causing NPB to lose its monopoly. In order to compete favorably, NPB needed to create more programs, and if possible, step up to graduate training. I was particularly interested in the graduate training idea because it was the only sustainable way I saw to produce qualified staff for our undergraduate programs.

The first challenge was that with the status of a polytechnic, NPB could not run master's programs on its own. The second challenge was that even if we found a way of running master's programs, we did not have the staff to teach these programs. True to my nature, I designed a solution. The new Bamenda-Enugu highway had made it possible to travel from Bamenda to the Nigerian border at Ekok in three hours. From there to Calabar was another three to four hours, making the whole journey from Bamenda to Calabar Nigeria the equivalent of traveling from Bamenda to Yaoundé, the capital of Cameroon.

I figured that if we negotiated a memorandum of understanding with the University of Calabar Teaching Hospital for the clinical component of our graduate programs and enlisted adjunct professors from the cream of professors we had in the College of Medical Sciences at Calabar and the Faculty of Health Sciences in the University of Bamenda, we would have pooled enough resources to convince the University of Buea to upgrade our Bachelor's degree mentorship agreement to include Master's programs. That was quite a stunt, but I pooled through with my share of the work.

In collaboration with my rector, director of academic affairs, and the wonderful project focal point in Calabar, we secured the memorandum of understanding with the University of Calabar Teaching Hospital, designed the curriculum for six masters programs in nursing, public health, and laboratory medicine, and obtained a rich staff list for these programs. All this was packaged and presented to the University of Buea for review and eventual approval after all the normal protocol must have been followed and recommended changes made.

When the minister of Higher Education visited NPB in December 2015 and announced that the National Polytechnic Bamenda had been upgraded into a University Institute, I saw it as a sign that our project had received a go-ahead from the Minister, since the change of status now provided a suitable structure for the implementation for those programs.

While I was busy with the Berlin and Calabar projects, running my faculty, and teaching my own fair share of courses, I won a scholarship from the Foundation for the Advancement of International Medical Education and Research (FAIMER) in the USA, to undergo a two-year graduate fellowship program in Medical Education, Research, and Leadership. I did my fellowship at the Sub-Sahara African FAIMER Regional Institute in Cape Town South Africa. The work-based nature of the program meant that I completed the theoretical modules online, using my experiences from work to write all my papers. This work-based training and online learning were blended with three short stays in South Africa, after which I completed the program in June 2016.

It is upon my return from South Africa that I was greeted with my unexpected appointment as Founding Rector and President of Jomatt Polytechnic. I put together the most qualified, talented, visionary, and dedicated team I could find and we relocated to Batibo with the goal of setting up and running the most disruptive institution that would serve as a reference for professional higher education in Cameroon.

Six months into my new dream job, and one month after welcoming our first cohort of students on campus, the series of strike actions began. First, it was the lawyers who went on strike demanding the restoration of the Common Law system in Anglophone Cameroon. Then the teachers went on strike demanding an end to the assimilation of the Anglo-Saxon education system by the French-dominated Yaoundé regime. Then came the civil society protest against bad roads and lack of basic amenities, championed by the famous "Coffin March" of Mancho Bibixy.

The government reacted to the protests with a heavy hand. I recall the day I miraculously wriggled through a crossfire on my way from work and ended up trekking for five miles in the midst of tear gas smoke to get home. The ruling party went on national television and poured propaganda after propaganda, sent delegations to buy off leaders of protesting groups, and staged counter-demonstrations in support of the Yaoundé government. Soon, overt violence broke out and people started dying.

The government outlawed the civil society movements, began mass arrests and torture, and shut down internet connectivity in the North West Region and South West Region. Almost every day, and for several weeks, we received text messages from the Ministry of Post and Telecommunications threatening huge fines or imprisonment to anyone who was caught "spreading false allegations against the government". Trapped in this chaos, I devised the habit of traveling to Mbouda in the French-speaking West Region every Monday, just to use the internet. As the situation kept brewing and more and more people kept disappearing, I used the narrow window of opportunity I had left to negotiate my escape.

10

Chapter 10: Walls in the Promised Land

Looking back on my life, it is apparent that I was born to lead. I used to be a ferocious reader when I was in my 20s. My faith, my sense of purpose, and my vision in life had been greatly shaped by the life and works of great American luminaries like Abraham Lincoln, William James, Benjamin Franklin, Malcolm X, Martin Luther King, and Ralph Waldo Emerson. America was indeed, the City on the Hill that represented the best of humanity. Although I considered myself to be a patriot who was bent on building my life back home and being a force of transformation in my country, I always looked up to the "Land of the free and home of the brave" as the evidence of what humans can accomplish, and the blueprint for what we could build in our own nation.

So, you can imagine my consternation when I entered the USA in June 2017. The White House was building a border wall, launching an assault on immigration, spewing lies, sabotaging international treaties, and fueling hate crimes. I was in exile in a land that was brewing with uncertainty. So, my only hope was to draw from my leadership genius and lead myself in preparation for my natural duty of showing the way to the many people who depended on me. Here is how the leader in me was born:

In 1998, I came home for the summer holidays after my first year in high school in Saint Joseph's College Sasse. As usual, we the young students of Mbatu were looking forward to the cultural week of the Mbatu Students' Association (MBASA). The student cultural week was an exciting annual event, packed with activities like sports, excursions, academic debates, symposia, drama, music, dance, cultural displays, community volunteering, and a gala night.

The Mbatu Students' Association was a community organization that brought together young people of Mbatu origin who were schooling anywhere in the world, from secondary school to university. The annual cultural week was the point of convergence of all MBASA members from around the country. Apart from providing a great opportunity to network and make friends, it was the sole platform for interaction with the community and its traditional, religious, and civil authorities.

The student associations of neighboring villages like Nsongwa and Chomba were often invited for sporting activities and galas. Parents and community leaders were often invited to give educational talks during the symposium night and to donate money during the gala. Funds raised during the gala served as the means of financing the activities of the association.

The Mbatu Students' Association has been a great incubator of leadership. Among its pioneer presidents is Samuel Mbigha, the founder and president of Progressive Comprehensive High School, the most populated and prestigious private academic establishment in Mutengene in the South West Region of Cameroon, and William Njim, a retired secondary school principal and current municipal councilor for Njimafor Mbatu at the Bamenda II Council. The peak of the association's glory days was during the leadership of Fidelis Nji Tita aka Doctor D, one of the most vibrant, most talented, and funniest young men I ever knew.

Doctor D was president of the association, a key player in the football team, author, director, and lead actor in many of the plays that were acted on stage. He was a magnetic personality that gave each event a natural charm you would not want to miss. In the early 90s, Doctor D graduated from University and relinquished office. By 1998 when I was moving from Lower Sixth to Upper Sixth in Sasse College, the term of office of the John Che Sarakang team had come to its end. He was eligible for re-election, and we all came that summer expecting to re-elect him, but he didn't make it home that year. Apparently, he was caught up that year in the transition from University to the "school of hard knocks".

The executive members present in Mbatu that summer did something quite unexpected. Under the leadership of Fon Asongwe and Immaculate Fonmedig, they convened what was supposed to have been a preparatory meeting for the cultural week, and during that meeting, they suggested to those in attendance the idea that since this was a transition period during which a new government would be elected, it would be great if a new team was constituted to organize and run the cultural week to test their level of preparation to take over leadership of the association.

It was a kind of a leadership internship in which the junior team would work as an actual executive for two weeks, under the supervision of the senior team. That sounded like a bright idea. It meant that one could actually be president for at least two weeks, without being intimidated by the weight of leading such a great organization because the big brothers and sisters were there to make sure nothing went wrong.

So, when I was nominated for Acting President, I accepted without blinking. My team and I, with excellent coaching from the outgoing leadership team, organized and executed a cultural week that was successful beyond expectation. By election day, I had scored enough points to run for president. And I won with an overwhelming majority.

I served the Mbatu Students' Association as President from 1998 to 2004 when I handed over to Fontinglet Elijah Cho. Many people thought I did extremely well, but what they did not know was that it was not so hard to lead a well-established organization that had deep-rooted traditions. So long as you were charismatic enough to mobilize people and keep them together, much of the agenda was already set. I however left a mark in a few places.

I led an excursion to the Mankon Fon's Palace, where we spent a day with the students of Mankon and Fon Angwafor III and amongst other things talked and laughed about the historic breakaway of the Mbatu Fondom from the Mankon Kingdom in a century and a half ago. I gave a memorable speech at the annual convention of the Mbatu Cultural and Development Association holding on the campus of Government Bilingual High School Mbatu, in the presence of His Royal Highness the Fon of Mbatu and Professor Beban Sammy Chumbow who was then the Rector of the University of Dschang. It was after that speech that I attracted the complement "brilliant young man" from Professor Chumbow, and the Fon assured me of his commitment to work with young people like us who were taking the community into the future.

Here is the problem with traditions. They are resistant to change, no matter how positive the change is. The two innovations I initiated during my six years in office were the Magazine project and the Scholarship project. I argued that as a student association, our natural vocation was education. The magazine was a platform we could use to hone in the creative writing skills and talents of our members and put on paper such treasures as the history of the Mbatu people, cultural and traditional institutions, and practices of the Mbatu people, and the Oral Literature of the Mbatu people. A section was to be dedicated to the biographies of great Mbatu people who we wanted to celebrate and hold up as role models for the young, and there would be more than enough room for creative material that young people loved.

By studying the cash flow of the association I figured that if we cut down on spending and made occasional appeals to parents to subsidize the funds we raised during galas, we would be able to save enough to offer scholarships to Mbatu children with brilliant academic records but with acute financial needs. In the Mbatu I grew up in, people barely survived. Back then, you could group most of us in the United Nations index of people who lived on less than a dollar a day. So we were poor people. But even among the poor, we had the poorest of the poor. Creating a scholarship fund for needy children was something even the Mbatu elites and the Mbatu Cultural and Development Association had never done.

We faced stiff resistance from some elites who not only refused to give us money but advised that it was fundamentally unacceptable for students to give scholarships to students. I responded that we were meeting a need and that the only argument they could use to convince us that we shouldn't be doing it, was to do it themselves. Of course, they didn't, and that gave us the excuse to defy them and move on with our plan. It took six years of fighting to establish these two new traditions, the magazine, and the scholarship fund, and I am eternally grateful to Elijah and his team who not only made my legacy their own but made it flourish.

In October 1999, I was admitted to study Medical Laboratory Science in the Faculty of Health Sciences of the University of Buea. Coming from Saint Joseph's College Sasse, my natural landing place was the Catholic Community of the University of Buea (CCUB) which the then Bishop Pius Suh Awa of Buea Diocese had created.

The bishop's motive for creating the CCUB was simple. There were thousands of students at the University of Buea, the lone Anglo-Saxon university in the country at the time, who were graduates of great Catholic Secondary schools around the country. It would be a great waste if these children from great homes and great schools entered the public university and got lost in the moral and Christian upbringing because they had no guidance.

The CCUB was created to fill this gap. It was a pseudo-parish attached to Saint Charles Lyonga Catholic Church in Molyko Buea. The bishop erected a community-building containing offices, library, and conference room, and appointed from amongst his priests, the finest people who worked as chaplains of this vibrant catholic student community.

Due to the death of my brother and sponsor Doctor Tamu, my final year in Sasse had been very hard both emotionally and financially. I had made a dramatic entry into the University and was living under terrible conditions. My brother's widow had moved out of their former apartment into a two-roomed apartment in an old wooden building, the type of houses called *calabot* in coastal towns in Cameroon. Because she had brought her younger sister and niece from the village to live with her and go to school, I was the odd guy in the house among three ladies. We packed the furniture in one living room, used the remaining room as the bedroom, and cooked on the veranda.

The three ladies used the family-sized bed while I slept on a mattress on the floor. Here was an adorable young woman whose husband had died unexpectedly, leaving her with nothing, and here she was still taking care of me because she loved the man too much to let his dreams die with him. I lived with her and successfully completed my first year of university studies. By the time I came back for the second year, Christopher had made arrangements with his friend Mbang Joseph for me to move in with him. The interesting thing was that Mbang Joe lived on the very same block that my sister-in-law was living in. So, when I moved out of the house, we still remained neighbors.

Mbang Joe and I bonded quite easily because his life was not complicated. The most valuable possessions in our room were the books on the reading table. Apart from the small bed, clothes stand, and kerosene stove, there was nothing else in the room. Have you ever wondered how a room can be too big for two people? It was so empty that when the moon shone at night we would get light in through the holes on the walls. There was a modern hostel right behind our *calabot* hostel and most times when the girls came in late and I was up studying, I could see their movements through the wall and hear all their conversations. I often wondered if we were on the same planet, let alone the same university.

All the tenants in the wooden section of Melrose Garden, as my hostel used to be called, plus the landlady's family, shared one external bathroom and two toilets. The difference between this community and boarding school was that you couldn't just jump into the shower while someone else was there. You would have to wait. One day, while waiting, I decided to count how many of us were actually using that one shower and two toilets, and it turned out we were sixteen.

When I was living with Evelyn, my late brother's young widow, and her sisters, my coping mechanism was to leave the house every day as early as possible and come back as late as possible, except on days that I had a specific assignment to do in the house. When I lived with Mbang Joe, our kerosene stove was more or less a decoration. Cooking was not part of our routine because there was nothing to cook in the first place.

One of my cousins William eventually rescued me in my third year by providing me sponsorship for the remaining two years of my undergraduate program. Finally, I got to live in my own well-furnished room in a proper hostel as a temporary reward for my resilience and academic prowess. The relief was temporary because even before graduation, William had backed out of his sponsorship engagement as a result of a petty family quarrel.

In case you are wondering where I got food from, there were four ladies who accounted for more than half the food I ate during all my stay at the University of Buea. Glory was a family friend and a big sister, Rose and Prudence were my classmates and study partners, and Irene was my sweetheart at the time. I say this with utmost sincerity, humility, and gratitude. These four ladies literally speaking, accounted for more than half the quantity of food I ate while in the University of Buea.

It is against this backdrop that I faced life at the University of Buea. The CCUB was more than a consolation. It kept me busy and distracted from my troubles. I had noticed that many people came early for Holy Mass on Sundays and just sat in church doing nothing until Mass started. I wrote reflections and obtained permission to read them out in church on Sunday mornings before Mass. Before long people started giving me positive feedback which kept inspiring me in such a way that week by week, both the content of my reflections and my oral presentation style got better and better.

Soon, people started requesting written copies. During that period, the then CCUB executive headed by Paul Itoe and Melanie Kesiki founded and launched THE SEED, the first official weekly bulletin of the CCUB. I was nominated as the pioneer editorial board, and an entire page was dedicated to my reflections.

The fame that The Seed brought me culminated in an unexpected happening. I was elected President of the CCUB for the 2001-2002 mandate. During the same year, back at the Faculty of Health Sciences, we had founded the Health Science Students' Association (HESSA) and I had been elected its pioneer Academic Affairs Officer. My office gave me the platform to create and launch THE CALL

FOR EXCELLENCE, a small weekly publication that provided inspiration, motivation, and academic advice primarily for younger students.

Our HESSA executive started the tradition of sending student delegates to attend professional meetings and scientific conferences, and I remember we created quite a sensation at the Annual Scientific Conference and General Meeting of the Cameroon Association for Medical Laboratory Sciences, in 2001.

Back in the CCUB, life was blissful. At the age of twenty, I was the youngest person ever to carry this amazing community on my shoulders. The three past presidents I had known, Julius, Dickson, and Paul were all older men who had come to the university after having spent some time working or teaching, as was the tradition in their day. They were experienced, they were elderly, and they had stamina.

Leading a university catholic community of almost five thousand students from different backgrounds, required more than age and experience. If God was not in your leadership then you were doomed. There I had an advantage. My deep personal issues had turned me into a deeply rooted spiritual person, my writing and speaking had built a connection between me and the community, and I was so innocent, humble, and outgoing that I loved everyone and almost everyone loved me without feeling threatened by anything.

The only time people really saw a president was when I was chairing executive meetings or giving official speeches. The rest of the time I was just the good guy who had a smile or a kind word for everyone. By the time my team headed by me and Della Bih, handed over office to the new executive headed by Dieudonne Kum and Jessie Bawak, we had launched the project for the construction of an autonomous parish for the Catholic Community of the University of Buea. Bishop Awa had promised me that this parish would be the best church he had ever built in his life as Bishop because he wanted CCUB to be his most important legacy. He had secured a plot of land next to the University campus, and the construction plans had given an initial estimate of 150million Francs CFA.

While counting on support from external sources, we were determined that the student community would take the lead in building this church. After several years of fundraising in and out of Buea Diocese, and after a tedious and meticulous execution of the project, Saints Peter and Paul University Parish was finally inaugurated by Right Reverend Bishop Pius Suh Awa before going on retirement. When I returned to work in Buea in 2007, worshipping in that church engendered an unfathomable feeling of gratitude and self-actualization.

During my years as a leader in CCUB, a small family emerged out of CCUB that would have a lifelong impact on me. There was this strange group of girls, namely Marie Chantal, Etchi Bessem, Mary Christie, Nadine, and Annie, whom I met every time I went to church on weekday evenings and weekends, for functions related to my office. We gradually became friends, and one day I accepted their invitation to join them in a prayer session. From that day I never left them again. They became my sisters and coaches who prayed for me and with me, gave real-time criticisms of my policies and activities, volunteered on every project my team was carrying out, and basically got things done.

We eventually adopted the name Fifi for this family, after a childlike and playful character in a cartoon that the girls loved very much. I had never lived in a home with a TV in my life till then, so I did not know what they were talking about. I just went along with the flow their luminous spirits created. The Fifi's were my spiritual, emotional, and physical powerhouse.

When my family came from Bamenda to attend my graduation in December 2003, they wondered what strings I had pulled to have such a grandiose graduation party. Well, that was the handiwork of the Fifis. All of these girls had secret ambitions of going to the convent after graduation. Without knowing it, these nuns turned me into a monk and before I knew it I was out of the university without knowing the other side of university life.

In 2013, one year to the silver jubilee of the creation of my former secondary school, Government Bilingual High School Mbatu, I successfully pulled off a stunt that had eluded many people before me for long. Ever since the first batch graduated in 1994, discussions had been held and efforts had been made at various levels to create an ex-students' association for the school. It took me one year to lay the groundwork, and when I had the audacity to call the first national convention in 2013, it became obvious that the GBHS Mbatu Ex-students Association was going to be formally created, even if there were only three people present. And in my immediate network, I had more than ten people I could count on. Achatoh George from London, Achu Kizob Richard from Accra, and Taku Claude from Yaounde, who were my seniors by two years in school, teamed up to back my move.

Now was the perfect time to make a long-time dream come true. They called me and encouraged me. We set up an organizing committee that worked through emails. And on the day of the convention, they were all present, together with over fifty others who together went into history as co-founders of the Mbatu Ex-students' Association.

At face value, an ex-student association of a government secondary school located in a remote village is not much to write home about, within the context of a long tradition of big names like the Sacred Heart Ex-students' Association (SHESA), Bali Old Boys Association (BOBA), Our Lady of Lourdes Ex-students Association (LESA), not to talk of Sasse Old Boys Assessment (SOBA) the elite group I naturally belonged to by virtue of having attended high school in Sasse.

GBHS Mbatu was created in 1989 to decongest GBHS Bamenda. The students of that school were the finest and smartest boys and girls you could find anywhere, but whose families did not have the economic strength to send them to the private schools. Some students trekked for up to ten miles to get to school and ten miles to get back home each day. The few whose parents could afford to rent rooms for them lived in the mini-hostels that cropped up in the community and were fed for the most part by the loving and charitable mothers in the community.

We went to Mbatu before the era of the proliferation of schools. Our stories are not only unique. Our bond is so strong, and people had been longing to reconnect to the point that once the association was formed, the response from past students all around the world was overwhelming.

We forged a partnership with our *alma mater* that would provide a framework within which we could become active developmental partners to the school.

We initiated an award program that recognized and celebrated the founding principal and staff of the school, to continue annually with awards to outstanding teachers.

We initiated a scholarship and academic excellence award scheme through which we provided school fees and didactic materials to over one hundred students in the first year.

We initiated an annual tour of primary schools in the surrounding villages to give academic orientation to students preparing to enter secondary school.

We started a charity initiative that took us to an orphanage where we spent a whole day singing, dancing, playing, inspiring, and sharing gifts we had brought.

We built a solid social support system for members that ensured that whether a member was in need, grieving, or celebrating, we were there.

We currently have four active MBAESA chapters in Cameroon plus a diaspora chapter. We named the 2015 convention "Pa Nyah's Weekend" after Mr. Nyah John Njeko, the pioneer principal of the school who is now in his late seventies. It was through his acceptance speech at the Lifetime Achievement Award offered to him by MBAESA, and the word of thanks that his family addressed to us after the occasion, that we knew that this kind gesture had turned out to be the highest point in the life of this great man.

Pain drove me into the contemplative life. Through contemplation, I learned resilience and empathy. Resilience and empathy propelled me into leadership. And leadership has become a vehicle through which I stay resilient while helping others to navigate the tough times in their lives.

Chapter 11: Black Lives Matter; My Life Matters

The George Floyd murder was indeed a turning point in American history. His dying words, "I can't breathe" were an echo of the aching souls that have been choking under slavery and systematic racism for the four hundred years that have passed since the first slave ships sailed off the coast of West Africa. When you are born in America as a black person, you have your own kind of problem. When you arrive in America as a black person from Africa, during a period when racism is at a fever pitch, you have a different kind of problem.

Racism used to be just a theory to me, and although, thank God, I have never been personally targeted by a hate crime, the fear was tangible, and sometimes, paralyzing. Whenever I went out jogging and I heard footsteps behind me, I would turn around and give way while keeping an eye on the person, just to make sure he had a friendly face. Whenever I heard a siren or saw a police vehicle, my heart would start racing before I had the time to tell myself that all was okay.

The danger of the Black Lives Matter movement, just like most social movements is that it easily becomes a vehicle for propaganda, misinformation, and even a business for some people. As the collective consciousness is focused on social messaging, we lose touch with the reality of what "Black Lives" really stand for. How can I see "Black Lives Matter" signposts everywhere but yet I am not feeling safe under my skin? How do we solve real problems in the lives of real people instead of keeping busy with the hype?

How can I stop feeling that I am just a number and get the assurance that I too, matter? What does it even mean to be "African American" these days? Does the immigrant who came in from Africa four years ago have the same story as the person born in America of parents who descended from great-grandparents who were shipped into America as slaves four hundred years ago?

As an educator and community leader, this too was a teaching moment for me. I reflected more deeply about what it means to be black in America. I reflected more deeply on the aspirations that people have when they decide to leave everything behind, even their families, to come to America. I reflected more deeply on the sacrifices that people make just to come to America. I reflected more deeply on the price that individuals and families pay on the altar of a racist world whose evil tentacles spread beyond America to the very fabric of the sham government, economic, religious, and educational systems we have in Africa.

I had left behind a country that was burning to the ground from the unforgiving fires of a wicket colonial past. And here I was, in the land where the wounds of slavery were being reopened by racism. Quite literally, to be black is to be in pain. But what do I do with my pain? Racism is a form of insanity that is rooted in a crisis of identity and community.

The problem with most people is that they waste their pain. They spend so much time comparing themselves with others, complaining about their circumstances, making excuses, and feeling miserable, that they miss the opportunity to take responsibility and shape the lives that the world is trying to shape them into. The survival mentality, the entitlement mentality, and the victim mentality all create a paradigm in which people interpret their life challenges negatively, and therefore are forced to react to them rather than act on them.

Because people depend on social conditioning to define their identity, the turbulent external world results in a shifting sense of identity. Consequently, a deep sense of insecurity sets in, forcing people to choose their communities based on fear and the need to numb the pain and emptiness within. This is how adolescents find themselves succumbing to peer pressure, join gangs, indulge in alcohol, drugs, and other practices that become deep-rooted addictions by the time they become adults.

We often do not realize that our habits and addictions are the major drivers of our choices and paths in adulthood. The young man who lives for beer and cigarettes will not waste his time solving calculus and waiting to earn a degree after three or four years, if he has figured out how to use the internet to make money for his beer and cigarettes, and have enough to spare in impressing girls.

The girl who looks pretty but has never received the love and appreciation she needs to cultivate self-confidence and focus and grow into a strong independent woman, will fall in the arms of every man that shows her love, no matter how fake. Wife battery in Africa will not stop anytime soon because, in the university towns, it is common practice for girls to abandon the rooms their parents have rented for them, move in with boyfriends, do laundry and cook for these boyfriends, get abused by these boys, sometimes undergo forced abortions, and yet hardly ever summon the courage to break away and stay on their own even for a while.

To these people, the cure for a bad relationship is another relationship. They hardly realize that they are in a vicious circle of their own making. There are empowering communities and there are disempowering communities. Communities like the Mbatu Students' Association, the Catholic Community of the University of Buea, the Faculty of Health Science Students' Association, the GBHS Mbatu Ex-students' Association, and organizations of their kind, are what I call empowering communities.

By the time a child leaves home and gets into the world, whether it is boarding school at the age of ten or university at the age of eighteen, the family has the duty of ensuring that this child is entering an empowering community. Empowering communities have a sense of identity, a social responsibility agenda, a personal empowerment framework, and a platform of actions that help people to discover themselves, relate harmoniously with other people, and bring out the best in themselves.

Unfortunately, most families and our modern society at large do not pay attention to this need. Instead, our youths are buried in the illusion of edited photos on Instagram, fake friends and followers on Facebook and Twitter, and an overdose of entertainment from YouTube and cable television. The potential of these social networks in driving the propaganda of other people is sickening.

I have come to accept that community is key to the thriving of the human spirit. We are inadvertently what our environment makes us. Just like the quality of the soil determines the health of the plant, the quality of the community that raises us, determines the depth of our soul, the breadth of our mind, and the health of our body.

No matter how perfect the genetic makeup of a seed is, if you sow it on soil that is polluted or undernourished, that seed has no chance of growing into the best possible version of itself. The family is our first community, but by the time we enter adulthood, we realize that we have typically spent more than two-thirds of our lives outside our homes. This means that the communities we become part of outside our family circles contribute more in shaping our identity and life, than our family does.

The only thing that makes the family unique is that it provides the ground that we can always fall back to when all else fails.

Community is the place where the identity our parents have given us, is shaped and reinforced, or redefined.

Community is that place where we experiment with our natural abilities and traits and get to find out from our friends which of these abilities and traits constitute gifts and talents that we could cultivate into superpowers.

Community is the place where we are bombarded by other people's stories, their own backgrounds, their own preferences, their own characters, ideas and ambitions, and many other realities that are different from our own, thereby leading us to expand our perspective by asking questions.

Community provides the framework in which we notice other people's needs and find ways of reaching out and serving them, no matter how many troubles of our own we have.

And herein lies one of the greatest secrets I learned through service and leadership: when you immerse yourself in serving others and helping them meet their needs, the universe orchestrates itself to serve you and meet your needs in ways that you could never ask or imagine.

It was when I was busy helping others bring out the best in them, that the best in me found expression.

When Immaculate and her colleagues challenged me to serve as acting president of the Mbatu Students' Association in 1998, they did not know in their wildest imagination that they were sowing a seed for a leadership career that would grow beyond the confines of that association and that community. If I had shied away from that challenge, perhaps the world would never have known that there was a leader in me, and the thousands of lives I have touched would never have been exactly the same.

When I narrate my challenges, it is not to say that I regret them or that if I could turn back the hands of time I would change them. Far from it. I celebrate them because they made me who I am. I know from personal experience that if you do not squeeze the orange, you won't get the juice, if you don't break the egg, you won't get the omelet, and if you don't put the teabag in hot water, you won't get the tea to enjoy.

From every indication, life was set up in such a way as to break the me that my mother gave birth to, so that a greater me could be born. And the bridge between those two versions of me is what I call resilience. My community is my new mother and the world is my new family.

There is a saying that if you surround yourself with five wise people, you will be the sixth; if you surround yourself with five millionaires, you will be the sixth; and if you surround yourself with five prostitutes, you will be the sixth. Well, if that law holds true, then what in the world would I not become by surrounding myself with thousands of happy people, thousands of saints, thousands of intelligent people, thousands of hardworking and creative people?

When I look at people who are occupied with only themselves, I feel sorry for them. I wish they knew that self-preoccupation is actually the cause of all their woes. The communities in which I have grown, have transformed a troubled child into a vibrant adult, a timid soul into a leader, and a wretched youth into a prosperous man. My path would have been different had I not had a community that gave me purpose.

My sufferings and inner conflicts would have ruined me had I not had a community that supported me. My potentials would have remained untapped had I not had a community that made room for these potentials. As I write these words, there is no sadness or trouble that can last in my mind for a minute without me finding someone to talk to.

Even when it comes to money, I live without fear because of the confidence that if the worst were to happen, there are hundreds of people out there who would rather go hungry than eat, knowing that I am hungry. My life is without burdens, for I feel like a drop in a happy ocean. Love is the only substance in my soul. If you are a sensitive person you will feel it even in my words on paper.

I feel that my life is a perfume that I am here to just pour out on everyone in the world, because without the unconditional love I have received, I am nothing.

I am proud of my black skin, and I strive to love everyone as I love myself, irrespective of the color of their skin. I love to call myself the ancestor of the human race, because that is what I am as an African. I celebrate diversity because I see it in the same way that I see the diversity of flowers that make a beautiful garden.

The source of my resilience in the face of racism is found in my deep knowledge of the fact that we humans are not our bodies. We are spirits that are inhabiting these bodies. Therefore, at a fundamental level, we are all one. Even at a physical level, the genetic differences that account for racial diversity do not count up to as much as 0.01% of the entire human genome. Racism is a denial of one's humanity and a celebration of pathological ignorance. When you know this, your response to a racist will be empathy, not hate, and certainly, not self-victimization.

12

Chapter 12: An Apocalyptic Pandemic

When the COVID-19 pandemic broke out, it was not just a virus that was infecting and killing people. It was the first outbreak of its kind that anyone alive had ever seen. The lockdowns caused businesses to fold up and millions of people became unemployed. Healthcare systems in Europe and America were brought to their knees, revealing the stark truth that the concept of advanced healthcare systems is for the most part an illusion.

Since Africa is the most religious continent on the planet, you can imagine how pastors and "prayer warriors" started seeing visions and making prophetic declarations. While battling with the rapid changes that I was experiencing in a COVID-stricken America, I did not abandon my role as a community leader. I created a Mobile Application to help people understand and practice safety precautions. I conducted surveys and focus group discussions on various topics relating to COVID-19.

I invested a lot of time publishing scientifically researched updates within my social network as a means of educating my community. Many times I came under fire for challenging the "men of God" or for not agreeing with the conspiracy theories. But I was not deterred because I knew that it was only a matter of time before scientific truth prevailed over conspiracy theories and prophetic visions.

As the Coronavirus COIVID-19 pandemic rages on, many experts are voicing their fears that both the infection and the lockdown measures that have been imposed worldwide as a means of controlling the spread, may lead to an explosion in mental health disorders. These fears are not utterly unfounded. Many public health and mental health experts are already actively involved in researching the mental health implications of the pandemic, the lockdown measures, and the economic ramifications.

This chapter is a synthesis of some scientific research articles and newspaper reports on this subject (as of the Spring of 2020). The aim is to give you a broad picture of what mental health disturbances you should watch out for in yourself, your family, and your community. The state of sustained stress is what we cannot do anything about. But watching out for the signs of anxiety and depression and taking timely action could save lives. Better still, knowing how to prevent anxiety and depression will avert the danger that lies ahead in terms of the potential mental health consequences of this global challenge we are currently facing.

People are anxious, stressed up, and worried about their family members.

Wang and colleagues have a wonderful research article in the *International journal of environmental research and public health*, in which they report that people are anxious, stressed up, and worried about their family members. According to this study, women and youths show higher levels of stress, anxiety, and depression, and people who are actively practicing precautionary measures are less anxious.

People who receive reliable information about the pandemic and are actively practicing precautionary measures are less likely to feel stressed.

"A survey was conducted to assess the Immediate Psychological Responses and Associated Factors during the Initial Stage of the 2019 Coronavirus Disease (COVID-19) Epidemic among the General Population in China. 1210 respondents from 194 cities in China were interviewed. In total, 53.8% of respondents rated the psychological impact of the outbreak as moderate or severe; 16.5% reported moderate to severe depressive symptoms; 28.8% reported moderate to severe anxiety symptoms; and 8.1% reported moderate to severe stress levels. Most respondents spent 20–24 h per day at home (84.7%); were worried about their family members contracting COVID-19 (75.2%); and were satisfied with the amount of health information available (75.1%). The study found out that female gender, student status, specific physical symptoms (e.g., myalgia, dizziness, coryza), and poor self-rated health status were significantly associated with a greater psychological impact of the outbreak and higher levels of stress, anxiety, and depression. Also, specific up-to-date and accurate health information (e.g., treatment, local outbreak situation) and particular precautionary measures (e.g., hand hygiene, wearing a mask) were associated with a lower psychological impact of the outbreak and lower levels of stress, anxiety, and depression."

An overabundance of misinformation on social media creates generalized fear and fear-induced overactive behavior.

Dong and Bouey, in their research article in the *Journal Emerging Infectious Diseases* about the public mental health crisis during the COVID-19 pandemic in China warn against what they term "a unique infodemic"—an overabundance of (mis)information on social media and elsewhere— which poses a major risk to public mental health during this health crisis. They write that as during the 2003 SARS and 2014 Ebola virus disease outbreaks, generalized fear and fear-induced overactive behavior were common among the public; and that both can impede infection control. They also reported that in addition, psychiatric disorders, such as depression, anxiety, and posttraumatic stress disorder, developed in high-risk persons, especially survivors and frontline healthcare workers.

World Health Organization experts are worried about a looming mental health pandemic as a result of the COVID-19 lockdown.
In her article in the *New York Post*, Melkorka Licea writes that COVID-19 may not be the only dangerous disease sweeping the globe because mental illness could also reach alarming levels during the coronavirus lockdown if not kept in check. She quotes Dr. Hans Kluge, the agency's regional director for Europe as having said the following: "We are definitely worried. We want to avoid a pandemic of mental disorders in addition to a pandemic of COVID-19."

Licea also quotes in her article, an Instagram post from an Iowa nurse Sydni Lane.

"I broke down and cried today. I cried of exhaustion, of defeat," "I have to go into every patient's room and in the back of my mind I think 'this could be the patient that gets me sick... that kills me.'

It is obvious that it is not only infected people that are afraid of dying, or family members that are afraid for their loved ones, or the general public finding it hard to adjust to the lockdown. The healthcare professionals who are at the forefront of the pandemic, saving lives, watching people die, and losing their colleagues, are battling with more mental and emotional trauma than we realize.

Are we enduring an involuntary psychological experiment?

Dr. Elke Van Hoof writes on the website of the *World Economic Forum* that the COVID-19 global lockdown is the world's biggest psychological experiment whose effects may be toxic if we do not take extra steps to mitigate them. He writes, "With some 2.6 billion people around the world in some kind of lockdown, we are conducting arguably the largest psychological experiment ever…this will result in a secondary epidemic of burnouts and stress-related absenteeism in the latter half of 2020…taking action now can mitigate the toxic effects of COVID-19 lockdowns."

Fear can be more harmful than the COVID-19

Researchers Ren, Gao, and Chen, in their article in the *World Journal of Clinical* Cases lament over the fact that discrimination, prejudice, and stigmatization, driven by fear or misinformation have been flowing globally, superseding evidence and jeopardizing the anti-severe acute respiratory syndrome coronavirus 2 efforts.

Here is an excerpt from a touching article in the March 26[th,] 2020 issue of the online newspaper India Today:

"On the night of March 19, panic gripped Delhi's Safdarjung Hospital when a person suspected to have contracted Covid-19 jumped to death from a seventh-floor window of one of its buildings. The 23-year-old student from Punjab was halfway through completing formalities for quarantine admission - soon after landing at IGI Airport from Sydney - when he took the extreme step. It took the police longer than usual to confirm his identity, perhaps because of the contagious nature of the disease.

"He and his mother had flown from Melbourne in the same flight. He had complained of fever and headache. His samples had been taken and sent for examination," said a relative. In South Delhi's Sukhdev Vihar, a 30-year-old man has started showing some worrying behavioral changes after his brother was found to be a Coronavirus suspect. He remained inside his room for two days and then suddenly exited from the family WhatsApp groups and started behaving indifferently. "When we spoke to him, he said he has put all his members on his 'black list'," said a family member....

...In neighboring Noida, a 60-year-old man has started showing similar traits after he came to know two weeks ago that his grandson is stuck in one of the virus-affected countries in Europe. "He wakes up in the middle of the night and screams out his grandson's name. We have a tough time making him understand that he is safe. The Doctor suggested we should keep him away from the news," said his son, who works with a real estate firm....

...These are not isolated cases. Stress has emerged as a new challenge in the time of Covid-19. Key triggers include escalating virus fears, complete isolation, the so-called social stigma and daily news of death & infection. Many feel worried about their relatives stuck abroad where the impact has been worse. Coronavirus cases in India climbed to over 600 on Wednesday which include 35 cases from Delhi. One patient has died and hundreds are quarantined. A 21-day nationwide lockdown kicked in from Tuesday midnight..."

South Africa's Government Response.

The Department of Health of the Republic of South Africa has officially recognized the need for the government to proactively address the mental health consequences of the COVID-19 lockdown in South Africa. The following statement is found on their website.

"Stress, anxiety, and a sense of isolation amid the global COVID-19 pandemic and South Africa's current 5-week lockdown can add to psychological distress, and for those already struggling with mental health disorders it is now more important than ever to keep up with treatment."

The lockdown may even affect lifespans, endanger students with special needs, and trigger a surge in domestic violence.

In their April 3rd, 2020 report on *Reuters*, Pell and Lesser expressed fears that a prolonged lockdown could affect not just mental health but life expectancy as well:

"The longer the suppression lasts, history shows, the worse such outcomes will be. A surge of unemployment in 1982 cut the life spans of Americans by a collective two to three million years, researchers found. During the last recession, from 2007-2009, the bleak job market helped spike suicide rates in the United States and Europe, claiming the lives of 10,000 more people than prior to the downturn. This time, such effects could be even deeper in the weeks, months and years ahead if, as many business and political leaders are warning, the economy crashes and unemployment skyrockets to historic levels...

"Already, there are reports that isolation measures are triggering more domestic violence in some areas. Prolonged school closings are preventing special needs children from receiving treatment and could presage a rise in dropouts and delinquency. Public health centers will lose funding, causing a decline in their services and the health of their communities. A surge in unemployment to 20% – a forecast now common in Western economies – could cause an additional 20,000 suicides in Europe and the United States among those out of work or entering a near-empty job market."

This April 11th, 2020 report on *ABP Live* captures the urgency and dimension of the mental health crises that the world may be facing as a result of the COVID-19 pandemic and lockdown measures.

"Anxiety, frustration, panic attacks, loss or sudden increase of appetite, insomnia, depression, mood swings, delusions, fear, and suicidal tendencies, have become quite common during the lockdown and helpline numbers have seen a surge in the number of phone calls they receive since the lockdown."

"People with preexisting psychological issues are unable to receive proper therapy on time or have had to go off prescription medication worsening their condition. The fact that E-prescription does not work is making it difficult to procure medication as chemists are supposed to keep a record of Schedule X drugs, psychological medication fall under this category."

"The lockdown has also seen a surge in the number of domestic violence cases, the worst affected are children & women who are now trapped inside their home with their abusers. Men who are either unemployed or frustrated about being home often taken to abuse their wives or children. SOS calls have risen ever since the lockdown."

The spectrum of mental health challenges and how they may be impacted by the COVID-19 pandemic.

I found an article by Megan McIntyre on the PSYCOM website in which she gives a beautiful overview of the nine major mental health disorders and how they may be related with the COVID-19 lockdown. I have gleaned and edited a section of the article for the purpose of this book, but I invite you to read the entire article on https://www.psycom.net/coronavirus-mental-health. You will find it to be one of the best crash courses on mental health that you ever read.

Anxiety and Coronavirus

While there are many specific types of anxiety, one of the most common is Generalized Anxiety Disorder (a.k.a. GAD), which affects estimated 284 million people worldwide. While it is normal to worry, those diagnosed with GAD have difficulty controlling worry on more days than not for a period of over six months and have three or more common symptoms: having a persistent sense of impending doom or danger, being irritable and on-edge, rapid breathing, constant trembling, feeling weak or tired, having difficulty concentrating or trouble sleeping, and having an increased heart rate.

For these people, the COVID-19 pandemic may create an elevated fear of catching or dying from the virus. Anxiety sufferers are prone to catastrophizing, which can result in behaviors like panic buying or trying different medications and treatments in an effort to "cure" or prevent coronavirus. They can also fall victim to compulsively checking the news, scrolling and scrolling for something more definitive that just won't come.

On the positive side, those who have been in treatment for an anxiety disorder might actually be better prepared for the current situation as they already have some coping mechanisms in place to deal with their day-to-day fears. But, for some, this could also be a tipping point that makes them paralyzed by that fear.

As frightening as the data is, we have to keep in mind that it does not even include the millions of people in developing countries that suffer from undiagnosed anxiety and other mental health disorders because mental health services are severely limited in these settings. Just to give you a hint, this author visited mental health service for the first time in 2017 when he moved to the United States.

Depression and COVID-19

While we all have bouts of sadness from time to time, for the more than 300 million people diagnosed with clinical depression worldwide, that grief and sadness is constant and comes with other symptoms like exhaustion, trouble sleeping, a shrinking appetite and/or overeating, sudden crying spells, and sometimes thoughts of suicide.

Just as with anxiety, the fear and isolation can be very dangerous for those with depression, because without an outside influence to remind them of the good, they may instead focus solely on the bad news and develop a skewed sense of the situation, and potentially not be able to pull themselves out of that spiral. Depression sufferers may have a growing sense of hopelessness or be paralyzed by their fear, leading them to neglect themselves and their health. Loneliness and fear can also be triggers for suicidal thoughts.

OCD and Coronavirus

Obsessive compulsive disorder is a type of anxiety disorder that happens when a person gets stuck in a cycle of obsessions and compulsions. Obsessions are considered any thoughts, images, or impulses that recur frequently and feel outside of your control to stop or manage. Compulsions are repetitive physical behaviors or thoughts that someone might use in an attempt to make their obsession go away. Most people with OCD are able to recognize that their compulsions will not make obsessions go away, but fall victim to them as they appear to be the only way they can cope or escape.

For those with OCD, specifically those whose obsessions and compulsions that revolve around cleanliness and germs, a global pandemic is their worst nightmare come to life. The CDC recommends hand washing and home sanitizing "frequently," but that can be taken to the extreme by those with OCD. Instead of washing their hands for 20 seconds every time they've been outside or coughed and sneezed, they may find themselves scrubbing their hands raw under scalding hot water for 20 minutes in an effort to feel "clean."

Substance Abuse Disorder and COVID-19

An all-too-common disorder that affects a wide spectrum of age, race, and socio-economic groups, substance abuse disorder is a disease that affects the brain and behavioral patterns, causing a person to be unable to control their use of addictive substances like alcohol, tobacco, illegal drugs, and prescription medication. Many people with a substance abuse problem also suffer from another form of mental illness—over 31 million adults worldwide, according to the most recent data from the World Health Organization.

The big concern for those in treatment for substance abuse is the risk of relapse. Many of those in treatment for substance abuse rely on daily meetings or support groups like Alcoholics Anonymous. While addiction is treatable, no one can recover alone. With isolation and lockdowns in place, many people aren't able to get the support they need to help battle their urges. Many other people who previously were not indulging in substance abuse may adjust negatively to lockdown stress by falling into substance abuse.

Eating Disorders and Coronavirus

There are three main types of eating disorders: anorexia nervosa, bulimia nervosa, and binge-eating disorder. People with anorexia tend to be obsessed with their weight, drastically restricting their calorie intake and extreme amounts of exercising, constantly thinking they are overweight even when they are in fact dangerously underweight.

For those with bulimia, their disorder is typified by periods of uncontrollable binge eating, followed by a sensation of being painfully full and the need to "purge" in an attempt to compensate or get rid of the calories they now feel guilty for consuming.

Binge-eaters will also experience that same urge to eat and inability to control how much they eat, but they do not practice purging or calorie restrictions post-binge.

For those with eating disorders, the main concern is around the perceived fear of lack of supplies. Those with an eating disorder may believe they need to hoard food; due to the consistently empty shelves they see at the grocery store. They may also find a reason to use these non-existent food shortages as an excuse to deprive themselves of food as a form of rationing.

ADHD and COVID-19

Attention-deficit/hyperactivity disorder (commonly known as ADHD) is a behavioral disorder that causes someone to suffer from inattention and difficulty focusing, along with hyperactivity, fidgeting, and impulse control issues. While most people relate ADHD to children, many adults also suffer from ADHD, which can lead to major disruptions in their daily life. This can include everything from work performance to relationships.

One of the main problems for those with ADHD who are stuck at home during the COVID-19 outbreak is a severe decline in productivity. With most people working from home and many companies having to lay off percentages of their workforce, now is not the time to look as if you are slacking on the job.

Another concern is that, due to their inability to focus or stay on task, some patients with ADHD may not be able to follow the strict guidelines for protecting themselves and your loved ones against the spread of infection. ADHD patients may forget to wash their hands frequently or find it hard to stay inside.

I am one of those who believes that social media addiction is playing an active role in promoting ADHD among adults. In Cameroon and the rest of African where very few companies use technology, "staying at home" is not synonymous with "working from home". Social media–induced ADHD is thus expected to take a toll the adult population in these settings.

Bipolar Disorder and Coronavirus

Bipolar disorder, (formerly known as manic depressive illness or manic depression), is a mental health disorder where people experience two distinct types of extreme emotional shifts identified as manic episodes and depressive episodes. When someone is having a manic episode, they experience what are considered "up" periods of emotions that include irritability, excitability, elation, and being energized. These are sometimes followed by "down" periods characterized by sadness, indifference, and hopelessness.

Like anxiety and depression, the stress and fear caused by COVID-19 can trigger these abnormal behaviors, specifically manic episodes, which can then be followed (although not always) but very intense depressive episodes.

Schizophrenia and COVID-19

Hallucinations, delusions, and impaired behavior are all symptoms of schizophrenia, a mental health disease that results in people being unable to interpret reality normally. They can act and speak erratically and may have trouble communicating or controlling some movements. They are also prone to suicidal thoughts.

For many of us, this strange new world we're living in due to COVID-19 can feel like some sort of alternate reality. For those suffering from schizophrenia, it creates a very dangerous situation, as their perception of reality can already be warped. People who have schizophrenia and are able to successfully function in their community most likely are able to do so through medication, a regular routine, and an array of support that could include physicians, caseworkers, and peer groups.

With COVID-19, all of this has been disrupted and they are now in a place of isolation that could make them a danger to themselves. If you are someone already prone to see the world through a paranoid lens, you may believe the misinformation about coronavirus that is circulating, or even be seeking it out to help make the news fit your version of reality.

Post-Traumatic Stress and Coronavirus

For anyone who has been exposed to a type of trauma, post-traumatic stress (PTS) is a common condition that can occur. It is most typically associated with military veterans, but is also something that can happen after traumatic events that range from car crashes and natural disasters to sexual abuse survivors. Symptoms of PTS include reliving the event (a.k.a. flashbacks), nightmares, avoiding certain places or activities that remind you of the trauma, paranoia, isolation, and hyperawareness.

The COVID-19 pandemic has created a strange new world in which people watch their loved ones being rolled away from their homes by heavily masked healthcare workers, people die in the Intensive Care Units without being surrounded by their loved ones, celebrities get buried with only a handful of family members present, doctors and nurses see more death in a week than they have seen in years, and TV channels now broadcast sometime as taboo as mass graves. For deeply religious people, it is hard to even begin to tell the degree of trauma that they may be going through as they experience the culture shock of watching their mosques, churches, temples, and pilgrimage sites being shut down. When religious beliefs and practices are disrupted, people get shaken at a deep level. Putting all of these facets together gives us a picture that PTS is no longer the "luxury" of military veterans.

3

Part 3: Understanding and Managing Stress

"The strongest oak of the forest is not the one that is protected from the storm and hidden from the sun. It's the one that stands in the open where it is compelled to struggle for its existence against the winds and rains and the scorching sun."
    ~Napoleon Hill~

Chapter 13: A Review of Human Needs

The Hierarchy of Human Needs

In his 1954 book, "Motivation and Personality" Abraham Maslow proposed the Hierarchy of Human Needs that has become a landmark in psychology and the social sciences. It is interesting to note that Maslow developed this theory based on his study of positive human qualities and the lives of exemplary people, much the same way that Napoleon Hill developed the Science of Success Course that was the basis of the bestselling book "Think and Grow Rich".

Over the decades, Maslow's theory has become the property of academics who use it to frame their intellectual jargons while paying little attention to actual solutions that create meaningful change in the lives of individuals. Using Maslow's Hierarchy of Human Needs as the basis of this book is a means of returning to the spirit of Maslow.

This book encapsulates a transformational perspective to mental health, as a means of empowering people with the knowledge, skills, abilities, and tools, that are required for the effective self-management of stress, thereby mitigating depression and its costly complications. Maslow ranked human needs into five ascending categories:

Physiological Needs

The physiological or bodily needs are the activities of daily living which include eating, drinking, bathing, clothing; the normal homeostatic functions of digestion, excretion, respiration, circulation; as well as basic needs like housing and energy. The physiologic needs constitute the elements that the body requires in order to function optimally.

Safety Needs

Safety needs address the need for one to be safe in one's environment by having their body, property, health, rights, and employment, protected. It includes intangible securities such as education and the freedom of speech and worship. The safety needs provide for mental wellbeing the same way that the physiological needs provide for physical wellbeing.

Love and Belonging Needs

This category of needs represents one's need for friendship, intimacy, and sexual union. It is the need for a person to feel bonded to another person. The love and belonging needs address the person at an emotional level.

Self-Esteem Needs

This category of needs reflects one's need to respect and be respected. It is one's sense of worth, value, confidence, or achievement in society. When the physiological, safety, and belonging needs are met, self-esteem is the natural outcome.

Self-Actualization Needs

Acceptance of facts, lack of prejudice, non-judgment, detachment, morality, creativity, problem-solving, and spontaneity constitute that category of human traits that may be termed spiritual traits. The term spirituality is very unpopular in conventional science, and this is the reason why despite its great strides on the material plane, science is still lame when it comes to adequately addressing the issues of human life as a whole.

The terms 'synchronicity', 'grounding' and 'flow' have emerged recently in the personal development literature to describe the state of being at one with the Source Field from which the material universe (and hence our bodies) originates, in which all things are sustained, and to which all things return.

In summary;

- Physiological needs address the physical body, and constitute the domain of clinical medicine.
- Safety needs address the mind, and constitute the domain of the social sciences, including psychology.
- Love and belonging needs address the emotions, and constitute the domain of psychiatry.
- Self-esteem needs encompass the physiological, safety, and belonging needs, which are collectively handled by the domain of mental health.
- Self-actualization needs belong to the spiritual plain of existence and are not part of main strain science. Because of this void, both clinical medicine and mental health fall short of being truly holistic, and it is no surprise that close to 300million people are estimated to be suffering from depression

worldwide while 1.5 million die each year as a result of complications of depression.

The Head, Heart, And Hand Model of Personal Transformation.

Although its roots can be found in the mid-20th century like Maslow's Hierarchy of Needs, it is only in the early 21st century that the Head, Heart, and Hand model became popularized in the education and business literature. The model was introduced by Orr in 1992 and expanded by Sipos, Battisti and Grimm in 2008. It shows the holistic nature of transformative experience and relates the cognitive domain (head) to critical reflection, the affective domain (heart) to relational knowing and the psychomotor domain (hands) to engagement.

This book is written to serve as a tool for personal transformation, and not just the clinical approach of managing symptoms. The head, heart, and hand modal is therefore being incorporated into this book as a blueprint to the transformation that you will need to undergo by engaging the three processes of critical self-reflection, empathy, and taking action.

By doing physical work, we secure our physiological needs. By doing mental work we secure our safety needs. By doing emotional work, we secure our belonging needs. When our physiological, safety, and belonging needs are met, our esteem needs are taken care of. Here, we see an interesting new model of living that weds Maslow's Hierarchy of Needs with the Head, Heart, and Hand model. This blended theory forms the philosophical basis of this book which you may consider as a course on resilience.

Chapter 14: The Origins of Stress

Stress is simply a disruption in the state of balance or harmony that the human body and environment require to thrive. Stress is part of our daily lives and constitutes the driver for our pursuits as we seek the satisfaction of ever-increasing desires. It is when stress is sustained, intense, and/or poorly managed that it leads to disease states.

Just as we have a hierarchy of needs, we can infer a hierarchy of stress:

- Physiological stress is a result of the deprivation of physiological needs.
- Mental stress results from the deprivation of safety needs.
- Emotional stress results from the deprivation of belonging and self-esteem needs.

- Spiritual stress results from the deprivation of self-actualization needs.

The following section gives an overview of each of these categories of stressors.

Deprivation of Physiological Needs

There are many events that can occur in the environment to either deprive people of their physiologic needs or significantly diminish their access to a reasonable amount and quality of their various physiological needs:

Shelter
Due to extreme poverty, there are millions, if not billions of people around the world who cannot live in decent houses. Even in this 21st century, there are people still living in shacks, under bridges, and so on. In some societies where family structures permit, many people live with extended family members and friends. There is a silent form of child trafficking that involves people sending their children to live with relations in the cities where they exchange manual labor for education or cash.

Children who live in other peoples' homes usually suffer various forms of stress ranging from discrimination, excessive labor, verbal abuse, physical abuse, even sexual abuse. Overcrowding usually creates a conducive environment for discomfort, self-consciousness, and easy spread of infectious diseases.

Food
Food insecurity is still a major developmental issue in the world. According to the WHO 2019 report, 820 million people are hungry globally. Lack of proper nutrition has severe consequences, espe-

cially on children. Impaired mental development, stunted growth, micro-nutrient deficiencies, and obesity are among the major clinical complications of lack of proper nutrition. Many people in the world do not have food because they are caught up in conflict, because they are living in drought areas, or simply because they do not have the money to afford it. The economic consequences of the COVID-19 pandemic and its lockdown control measures have only come to exacerbate an already bad situation.

Water

It is hard to imagine life without water. But if you are one of those who has so much water to drink, cook, bathe, do your laundry, and water your garden, you probably take the importance of water for granted. The amount of water you used in bathing this morning without even thinking about it is the amount of water some people trek for ten or more miles to fetch and preserve for drinking for at least a week. Access to potable water is still a major problem in developing countries. In some regions, the problem is made worse by natural causes such as droughts and climate change that is systematically drying up water sources. Again, poverty is implicated in water access in the sense that some people are stuck in dry places simply because they have nowhere else to go to.

Clothing

Clothing has been transformed by our capitalistic society into a lucrative fashion industry to the extent that we have lost sight of the fact that the ability to decently cover one's nakedness is a fundamental human need. There are millions of people around the world who do not have clothes and shoes to wear. While this does not matter to some indigenous communities where everyone is running around half-naked, it can be a serious problem when you live in modern society and you are always feeling self-conscious because of that one pair of shoes and one shirt that has become like a uniform on you.

Healthcare

Healthcare is a crucial physiological need because it involves all the interventions, both preventive and curative, that ensure that the homeostatic functions of the body are in optimal shape. Where people lack access to basic healthcare, whether due to financial, geographical or social barriers, the quality of life is severely impaired. Unfortunately, this is true for billions of people across the globe.

Deprivation of Safety Needs

You feel secure when you are able to function optimally as part of society. There are some needs that are as essential as the physiologic needs but they are not as tangible. Such needs include education, employment, communication, safety, energy.

Education

The illiteracy rate in the world is still alarming for the 21st century, especially in developing countries. In many developing countries women have limited access to education while in developed countries, minority groups are often the victims of limited access to education. Education is an essential ingredient to optimal living in the modern world, so when one is not educated, it poses a real threat to survival.

Communication

There is hardly anything one can do these days without using a telephone and the internet. Digital technology is rewriting the modern world in every aspect; trade, education, banking, transportation, leisure, you name it. It is obvious that in order to function optimally in the modern world, one's consistent access to affordable internet connection. In developing countries, internet coverage is still very limited, the cost is still too high and quality often poses a problem to the degree to which one can use it.

The COVID-19 lockdown gave birth to a new work-from-home boom. But, in reality, how many people are able to work from home? Communication is not only about phone and internet. Good roads are still a major problem in many countries and in developing countries, a car is still a luxury or status symbol.

Security

As a member of a community, a person is supposed to be able to move around freely without fear of assault or violation of their human rights and dignity. Where there are recurrent acts of violence, brutality, banditry, or abuse, the lives and property of people are no longer safe. This is a major stressor in the lives of people who live in communities where they are victimized by racial, political, or religious discrimination. In societies where women are not respected and can even be raped simply because they found themselves at the wrong place at the wrong time, it is hard to be a woman and feel safe.

Growing up in a neighborhood that is controlled by gangs is a stressful experience. Being an immigrant in a country where refugees are not welcome can be very painful whether or not a person has papers. Unfortunately, there are billions of people around the world who do not feel safe due to one or more of the above reasons.

Energy

Various forms of energy are required for cooking, heating, food preservation, powering automobiles and other engines that make life easier, and most importantly lighting. Whether it is firewood or gas, whether it is hydroelectricity or solar energy, a person must have a sufficient supply of the energy form that is most conducive for his/her environment in order to live a comfortable or decent life. This is however not usually the case for most people, especially in developing countries where power supply is either unavailable or erratic and where bills are usually a pain in the neck.

Freedom of worship and expression

In many places around the world, people are subject to abuse because of their religious beliefs, political affiliations, language, cultural practices, gender, and even the color of their skin. Where people do not feel safe, they live in a state of stress.

Deprivation of Love and Belonging and Self-Esteem Needs (Social Needs)

The love and belonging needs and the self-esteem needs can be grouped under social needs. While love and belonging belong to the Feeling domain, self-esteem belongs to the Ego domain. For the purpose of this course, both have been treated under emotional health.

Humans are social beings by nature. They require deep and meaningful relationships with other humans as a means of experiencing their sense of being. In the absence of genuine love and friendship, a person feels empty and unworthy.

Parental Love and affection

In homes where there are so many children, most kids feel lost in the crowd as the parents are preoccupied with providing the physiological and safety needs of the children and have no time to attend to their emotional needs. School makes things worse with large classrooms and so many students per teacher. Billions of children grow up feeling like a vacuum because no one is actually paying attention to them. When emotionally abandoned kids cluster together and start improvising their own reality, society complains about peer pressure. What those kids and every other human yearns for, is to be seen, heard, and felt, that is, to belong.

Friendship

Capitalism has influenced the modern way of thinking to the degree that it is hard to make a distinction between the words friendship and transaction. When humans were more innocent and less self-centered, you were certain that a person was your friend because they genuinely loved you and enjoyed sharing their life with you. Today, friendship is mostly transactional, and in western societies, this includes dating and marriage. People think more about what you have that they want, than they think about what they have to share. As people are busy trading material favors, the emotional self silently starves and withers like an unused muscle.

Sexual intimacy

As people mature into adulthood, the love and protection they get from parents and siblings, and the acceptance and identity they get from peers, matures to the need for an intimate, sexual, and exclusive relationship. In traditional societies where sexuality is still considered sacred, it is obvious that sexual intimacy plays a great role in keeping people happy, productive, healthy, and living longer. In western society, sexuality has been vulgarized and commercialized to the degree where it is hard to tell how deep relationships really go, even when sex and babies are involved.

Being valued as a person

While our physiological and safety needs cater for the health and comfort of our bodies and minds, our need for love goes deeper into the essence of our being. If we consider that the inner self is the real person and the body is just a container, then we will immediately recognize the crisis that arises when a person's life is void of love. In the absence of love, the inner essence of a person is not awakened. Such a person feels like he/she is just an object or a machine:

- At the workplace, the employee is often a machine that gets the job done and brings in the profits and gets paid;
- At home many women feel like they are just a machine that provides the sexual pleasure of their partner and takes care of the children and the house;
- The sports star or entertainment artist is usually just a machine that performs at its peak to please the fans and bring in the profit that the team or producer wants;

There are several other disruptions in human society that create an unhealthy environment in which people starve emotionally. The problem with emotional starvation is that it is not immediately visible. It builds up without notice, and often erupts only when it has reached a critical stage.

Deprivation of Self-Actualization Needs

Since most humans are still trapped in the race for survival a very tiny minority of humans ever attain the stage of self-actualization. The educational systems are designed for the mass-production of a labor force that will drive the economy. In educational circles, almost no one really talks about self-actualization or purpose in life. The multi-billion-dollar personal development industry emerged to fill this gap, but even there, most so-called teachers and mentors base their teachings on philosophies and methods that turn people into peak performers, rather than self-actualized beings. In other words, most of what the motivational industry does is to make the machines perform better.

Your identity

Beyond the physical, mental, and emotional self lies one's sense of identity or what we may call the essential self or spirit of a person. A self-actualized person is a person who knows who he/she is, and is living in the progressive realization of his/her purpose in life. This implies that the physiological needs have been met, the safety needs have been met, the love and belonging needs have been met, and the person is now soaring on the wings of self-knowledge, self-expression, and peace of mind or self-fulfillment.

Your gift

Every human being has a gift that he/she is here to bless the world with. The spontaneous overflow of your gift is the state known as self-actualization. In order to find your gift, you must first know who you really are. Your gift is often not something that is immediately related to what you studied in school or what you are doing for a living.

Your purpose

It is funny to imagine that humans came to earth just to wake up every morning to run around looking for money to come and pay bills. But the pressure to keep up with the bills is so great that most people hardly think of anything else. They are trapped in the maze of survival.

Everything in creation has a purpose. The purpose of the orange tree is to blossom into the most fruitful orange tree it can be. It is the same thing with humans. Meeting our physiological needs, safety needs, and belonging needs is just a means of creating the ideal conditions for our body, mind, and heart to play their role in aiding the inner being to live its purpose.

Spontaneous self-expression

Spontaneous self-expression is what is referred to as creativity. Humans are creative beings and it is only when you have started expressing your creativity that you can be said to be living life to the full. He who has not attained the state of creativity is still busy surviving. For example, if you have a gift for poetry, then your bliss lies in writing poetry. When you surround yourself with the conditions that make it possible to spontaneously express the poet in you to the benefit of the world around you, then you could be said to be self-actualized. It is immediately obvious that this state of being is not practicable if you are uneducated, unemployed, unable to meet your daily needs, and lack the emotional security of a loving relationship.

Bliss

Bliss is the perfume of self-actualization. It is when a person is naturally and spontaneously joyful that we say a person is successful. There is really no standard that one can use to determine what amount of physiological, safety, and belonging needs can be considered enough for a person. It is purely subjective. While one person needs a private jet, the other needs just a bicycle. While another needs just one loving wife and one kid, another may desire four wives and twenty children.

While one person desires just a roadside shop from which to earn a decent living, another desires to be the CEO of a multinational company. What determines the value of an object or experience is the degree of satisfaction that a person derives from it, rather than its intrinsic value. You will agree that a Ferrari has no value to a Pygmy in the rainforest of Africa or as Eskimo in the Arctic. There are far more happy people who are homeless than those living in mansions. The ultimate test for a self-actualized person is, therefore, not the number of external things they have accumulated but rather how joyful they are.

Materialism and spiritual starvation

Modern society is characteristically materialistic, shallow, and egotistical. The systematic sacrifice of the deeper need for purpose and self-actualization on the altar of survival and peak performance leads to a society in which people are chronically stressed because their lives feel empty and meaningless. This is a very dangerous place to be in.

Tragedy and shock

On some occasions, a sudden tragic event may occur that shakes a person to the core of his/her being. Natural or man-made disasters, heartbreaks, death of a loved one, abandonment by a parent, forced separation from parents, rape, unexpected termination of a job, a business deal that goes south, diagnosis of a life-threatening disease like cancer, etc., are among the many triggers that cause people to question the meaning of life, the meaning of their existence, and so on. The COVID-19 pandemic is by far the most cataclysmic global crisis of the 21st century so far, and to say that people are shocked would really be an understatement.

Persistent suffering

In many situations, people reach the stage where they give up on life only because they have suffered for too long and have come to the end of their road. When poverty, misery, or abuse is consistent, the deprivation of a person's physiological, safety, belonging, and self-esteem needs become a norm. This state of normalcy gradually deteriorates to despondency as the person's sense of resilience diminishes over time.

Chapter 15: How We Respond to Stress

As mentioned earlier in this book, stress is a normal response to either positive or negative stimuli in our daily lives. In a sense, stress is actually healthy. It is simply a signaling system to tell us that something has changed in our internal or external environment, thereby inviting us to take action to adapt, such as to protect ourselves. Understanding one's stress and developing proactive strategies to cope with stress is, therefore, a vital part of human life.

When stress is poorly handled, anxiety and depression may result. Unfortunately, most people are unaware of their stress dynamic and it is often only when they have developed mental health problems that they start seeking solutions, if at all they do. As is always the case, we find that prevention is better than cure. Empowering people with the skills to understand their stress dynamic and proactively manage their stress will keep many people out of depression and avert the many morbidities and mortalities that are engendered by depression.

Distress: Response to physiologic stress.

When a person's physiological needs are not adequately met, the state of distress is the result.

A distressed person is basically an uncomfortable person. Discomfort is so common that people hardly notice that it is a form of stress that often leads to more serious mental health issues if allowed to persist for long. The cycle of desire-satisfaction-desire is normal in human life. We all wake up every morning with the goal of making our lives more comfortable.

When an environment is conducive for the progressive improvement of a person's conditions in life to something more and more comfortable, then that person is in a state of health. When an environment is so hostile that one's basic needs are not met and one is forced to live in perpetual discomfort, say hunger, then that person is in a state of stress. When discomfort is allowed to persist for long, it degenerates into a more serious mental health issue.

So the thing to note here is that some form of distress or another is part and parcel of our daily lives. It is our distress that pushes us to seek a more comfortable and more expanded life. What is undesirable is perpetual deprivation – the situation in which people are unable to meet their needs because of hostile circumstances beyond their control.

Responses to distress

When people are uncomfortable on a consistent basis, the next thing is that they start worrying. For example, they worry about where their next meal will come from, they worry about when they will be kicked out of the place where they are taking shelter, they worry about how the next bill will be paid, etc.

An uncomfortable and worrisome person usually finds it difficult to focus on the present moment or on the task at hand. Since their thoughts are always buried in the memory of past discomfort and fear of future discomfort, they are often very distracted from current reality.

Worrisome and distracted people also have the tendency to be very irritable.

The feeling of uneasiness or embarrassment is also a common feature among people who are conscious of their lack of basic needs.

Adaptations to distress

There are two types of physiological stress: the flight-fight response that the body mounts to protect itself from danger, say when confronted by a snake or an accident, can be called *acute physiological stress*. The other type of physiological stress is the one in which the bodily response builds up more slowly but surely, due to persistent absence or shortage of the essential needs of the body like food, shelter, clothing, energy, water, etc. This can be termed *chronic physiological stress*.

When people live in conditions where they are consistently deprived of the basic needs they require to survive, they pass through the immediate response of distress and move to the stage of adaptation. It is here that they start manifesting tendencies such as greed, hoarding, cheating, and binging.

Greed

Greed is the selfish and excessive or intense desire to have more material things like food, money, etc. than one really needs. A greedy person is basically possessive of material things because he/

she has an unconscious fear of the absence of these things. Most of the time we judge greed on the surface, but when we look deeper, we will usually find its origins in some past state of chronic deprivation.

Hoarding

Hoarding is an obsession with things and constitutes one of the variants of greed. A hoarder piles up things that he/she does not need, and cannot explain why he/she is piling them up.

Binging

We are all family with those people who go to a party and eat enough food to last them a week, or youths who once they have started drinking, will not stop until the bar is empty. Binging is a very common tendency in all societies both affluent and poor. With the advent of movie series, people now binge with TV as well, since they won't stop watching a movie till they have completed the whole season.

Stealing

Some people resort to taking what belongs to others as a means of meeting their own needs. Stealing usually begins as the innocent childhood tendency to grab something that no one would otherwise give you, out of sheer survival instinct. But the more habitual it becomes, the more it takes root into a person's personality. Some people grow out of it as life gets better, but others never recover. They go on to become robbers, gangsters, or the white-collar gangsters we find in business and politics.

Fear: Response to mental stress.

When people are deprived of their survival needs, mental stress results. The state of mental stress is basically the state of fear. The common types of fear are:

Fear of failure

People are afraid to enter into relationships, apply for jobs, start businesses, make a speech, and so on because of the gripping fear that it will not work out.

Fear of the unknown

That which is familiar is the comfort zone for most people. The sense of self is often so fragile that people will rather remain in their comfort zone they know, no matter how 'uncomfortable' it is, than venture into some unknown territory. They feel safe, even in their pain because it is the only thing they know.

Fear of pain

People who have ever experienced pain naturally have their system programmed to avoid pain. This is the case especially with people who have in the past suffered injury or abuse. It can be physical or emotional.

Fear of loss

We are all too familiar with the paradox where a person is passionate about having a certain object or relationship, and then the moment they have it, that same passion becomes transformed into the fear of losing that thing or person. The fear of loss makes people behave in weird ways, although in their eyes they are being protective and loving.

Fear of rejection

The major reason why people fear failure is that in their minds, failure is synonymous with loss. This is especially true among people who are under peer pressure to maintain certain standards as a condition to deserve membership in a certain click. In a broader sense, people whose sense of self is attached to the ego and the social perks they received from society are terrified by the prospects of losing this social pride should they encounter defeat or failure in a certain venture.

Conditioned fear

A conditioned fear, also known as a phobia is an exaggerated, often illogical, and inexplicable fear for an object, a group of things, or an experience. The number of phobias that are now recognized by the psychological community is way above one hundred. Examples include Hypochondria (Fear of becoming ill), Aerophobia (Fear of flying), Aquaphobia (Fear of water), Acrophobia (fear of heights), and Erythrophobia (fear of blushing).

Response to Fear

The state of fear is the state in which a person feels insecure because of their awareness that something of vital importance is missing, or will become missing in their lives. Fear goes deeper than the physiological responses. It is a conscious awareness of deficiency. The survival needs are the needs that a person needs to function normally in the physical environment, but unlike tangible (physiological) needs like food, the survival needs are intangible, such as education, employment, safety, human rights, freedom to enjoy life, etc.

Just as the adrenaline rush is triggered to prepare the physical body for fight or flight when one is physically threatened, the mind has its own defense mechanisms that are triggered when one's survival is threatened by the absence of safety needs.

People respond to fear in various ways, the common ones being the feeling of inferiority,

- Avoidance
- Negative self-talk
- Anxiety
- Pessimism
- Procrastination
- Complaining
- Blaming
- Excuses

Adaptations to Fear

When the passive responses to fear become permanent, the mind naturally improvises a means of survival. People who live in chronic fear demonstrate tendencies such as:

- Bitterness
- Envy
- Cynicism
- Discouragement
- Nervousness
- Panic
- Substance abuse
- Self-sabotage
- Paranoia (including delusion and schizophrenia)

Depression: Response to emotional stress

Human beings are social animals. The fact that we are created for community means that it is through relationships that we gain our sense of identity, our sense of worth, and our sense of fulfillment. The types of relationships we cultivate can be distinguished along the lines of the eight kinds of love that have been postulated by modern psychologists.

Agape — Unconditional and universal Love.
Eros — Romantic Love.
Philia — Affectionate Love.
Philautia — Self-love.
Storge — Familiar Love.
Pragma — Enduring Love.
Ludus — Playful Love.
Mania — Obsessive Love.

Developmental psychology is the branch of psychology that studies human needs and behavior across the lifespan. Children rely on their parents and siblings for the fulfillment of their love and belonging needs. When they become adolescents their focus shifts to their peers. Later as they become young adults, and subsequently adults and seniors, they rely on their sexual partners and life-long friends for their love and belonging needs. Understanding this dynamic is a crucial step to identifying the vacuum in the life of a depressed person.

Depression results when a person experiences a consistent emotional vacuum. In the modern world, parents are too busy to give attention to their children. Even in homes with many children, sibling rivalry is an easy way in which the need for attention is demonstrated by children. In the community or at school, children and adolescents turn to their peers for a sense of belonging. If for some reason a child is excluded or ridiculed by his/her peers, this becomes a source of depression.

As people become older and ready for intimate friendships and romantic relationships, the lack of these or failures in relationships become a source of depression, especially among middle-aged adults.

People who experienced love and acceptance through all the stages of their development, that is from parents and siblings, from peers, from friends and partners, grow up to have a healthy sense of self-love which reflects on their relationship with others. Depression is common among those who were deprived at one stage or another, maybe because they grew up in broken homes or were maltreated by peers, or suffered abuse at the hands of those who were supposed to protect them.

We also have those who have developed an unhealthy sense of self-love due to the fact that they were pampered and spoiled as kids. These people indulge their ego to the degree that it feels like the only reason why other people exist is to make them feel good about themselves. When flattery is not forthcoming they sink into depression because they do not feel appreciated.

Conventionally, depression is categorized clinically into recurrent depressive disorder and bipolar disorder.

Recurrent depressive disorder: this disorder involves repeated depressive episodes. During these episodes, the person experiences a depressed mood, loss of interest and enjoyment, and reduced energy leading to diminished activity for at least two weeks. Many people with depression also suffer from anxiety symptoms, disturbed sleep and appetite, and may have feelings of guilt or low self-worth, poor concentration, and even medically unexplained symptoms.

Depending on the number and severity of symptoms, a depressive episode can be categorized as mild, moderate, or severe. An individual with a mild depressive episode will have some difficulty in continuing with ordinary work and social activities, but will probably not cease to function completely. During a severe depressive episode, it is very unlikely that the sufferer will be able to continue with social, work, or domestic activities, except to a very limited extent.

Bipolar affective disorder: this type of depression typically consists of both manic and depressive episodes separated by periods of normal mood. Manic episodes involve elevated or irritable mood, over-activity, pressure of speech, inflated self-esteem and a decreased need for sleep.

Response to Depression

Just as distress results in physical stress and fear results from mental stress, depression is the result of emotional stress. This means that just as the response to physical stress is seen in a person's bodily disposition, and the response to mental stress is seen in a person's mental attitude, the response to emotional stress can be seen in the person's emotional and psycho-somatic expressions. The common signs of depression are:

- Sustained sadness
- Sustained apathy
- Insomnia
- Too much sleep
- Persistent pains and aches
- Persistent digestive problems
- Change in appetite
- Disruption in daily activity pattern

Adaptation to Depression

The adaptations to depression can be considered as the things that people do subconsciously to cover up the void that has been left by their lack of love, acceptance, and belonging. In order words, a depressed person's adaptation mechanism is to do anything that will get him/her noticed. Some of these changes in lifestyle or behavior include:

Body piercing and tattooing

While we cannot say that everyone who engages in body piercing and tattooing is a depressed person, it is very likely that there are many people who pierce and tattoo their bodies because they want to become noticed or because they want to blend with a certain culture or peer group. The need to be noticed and the need to succumb to peer pressure are classic adaptations to depression.

Anorexia

Anorexia is a form of self-torture in which people starve themselves into losing weight due to obsession over the need to slim down. It usually has dire health consequences but the victim is not attentive to them because he/she is preoccupied with attaining the ideal shape and weight that will make him/her feel good and accepted.

Being possessive

Possessiveness is the emotional equivalent of greed and hoarding. It is inspired by the fear of losing the person we love. Mania or obsessive love is an extreme version of possessiveness.

Craving for attention

There are many ways in which people crave attention. Some people become loud and aggressive when they are among people. Some people are a nuisance to their neighbors. Some people over-dress while others move around half-naked. Even the car you drive could be a way of drawing attention to yourself. In this digital age, the fastest-growing outlet through which people crave attention is social media platforms like Facebook, Instagram, and Twitter. Social media addiction is increasingly gaining the attention of psychologists and psychiatrists.

Stressing out

Stressing out is a way of focusing the energies on the body to make up for the deeper feeling of emptiness. This includes workaholics (people who are addicted to work) as well as those who are obsessed with working out in the gym.

Anger/temper tantrums

Depressed people are not only very irritable. They flare up at the slightest event that threatens their frail sense of self. Some express their temper tantrums through violence while others express theirs through withdrawal.

Obsession

Depressed people have the need to take attention away from themselves and stay busy with external things. Obsessive behaviors like gambling, talkativeness, gossiping, and fanatical tendencies (religious fanaticism, political extremism, entertainment fanaticism, sports fanaticism, etc.) are some of the common outlets.

Bullying and superiority complex

Bullies are people who gain their sense of being by lording it over other people. Their ego feeds on their ability to make other people look and feel small. They are compelled to make themselves feel important in this way because otherwise, they feel inferior. Superiority complex is a silent form of bullying and really stems from a deep sense of insecurity.

Despondency: Response to Spiritual stress

The ultimate form of stress is what we may call spiritual stress. Of course, you won't find the term "spiritual stress" in psychology textbooks and journals, for the simple reason that conventional science limits itself to the superficial things that can be measured and manipulated. The inability of conventional mental health and psychiatry to tackle the spiritual roots of mental health problems accounts for the overwhelming failure of this discipline in solving the problems that people go through. To be spiritually stressed simply means to lack a sense of identity and purpose. This is the state of despondency or hopelessness.

There are three paths that commonly lead to despondency:

The first and most common path is the lack of a spiritual foundation due to the materialistic culture in which people are raised. This is the epidemic of the western world.

The second path is when a person goes into shock due to some sudden tragic event and does not recover from it.

The third path is when a person progresses from distress, fear, depression, and ultimately enters the state of despondency because his/her bitter experience of life has provided evidence that living is not worthwhile.

Response to despondency

Despondency is the end stage of depression and manifests in very obvious ways.

The expressions of despondency are the classic red flags of suicidal tendencies. These include:

- Researching ways to die or to kill
- Becoming obsessed with violence
- Being extremely aggressive

- Talking about:
    - Killing themselves
    - Killing someone else
    - Hurting themselves
    - Hurting others
    - Feeling hopeless
    - Having no reason to live
    - Being a burden to others
    - Feeling trapped
    - Unbearable pain

Adaptations to despondency

When the spirit is broken, the final defense mechanism is to end it all. Suicide is ending one's life physically. But there are many ways in which people tune out of life mentally, emotionally, and spiritually long before they ever end their physical life. These include:

- Sadistic behavior
- Masochistic behavior
- Psychopathic behavior
- Sociopathic behavior
- Craving risk or danger
- Dying by suicide

16

Chapter 16: Be the Change

When you are sailing through troubled times, the one thing that will keep you going is the assurance that the storm will pass and you will be just fine. The pilot keeps his plane in the direction of his destination airport and tears right through the turbulence. The sailor keeps his ship in the direction of his destination port and tears rights through the tides. In the same way, you must keep your attention on your future and shuttle right through the tough times.

But most people are so busy living hand-to-mouth that they have no time to think about tomorrow. No doubt, at the slightest provocation, they go financially and emotionally bankrupt, and some even commit suicide. Create a blueprint of your life so that you will have a big picture to focus on and give you a broader perspective of the seasons that come and go.

Create a blueprint of the lifetime version of yourself. If you were to be an invisible presence at your own funeral, what would you like to hear the mourners saying about you? What legacy would you leave in this world?

Create a blueprint of the long-term version of yourself. If you are now 40 years old like me, what would you plan to accomplish by the time you are 60?

Create a blueprint of the medium-term version of yourself. If you are now 40 years old like me, what would you plan to accomplish by the time you are 50?

Create a blueprint of the short-term version of yourself. If you are now 40 years old like me, what would you plan to accomplish by the time you are 45?

Create an immediate action plan for the things you can do today with what you have and under the given circumstances. Then, focus on doing it.

Resilience exercises

In this book, I have offered you an 8 step system that you can apply to cultivate resilience. I have used my personal life journey as a means of creating the immersive experience that you need to engage with these insights at a subconscious (emotional level). This is because no matter what knowledge you acquire if it does not go beyond your brain, sink into your body, and vibrate in your emotions, that knowledge cannot change you. Having given you knowledge for the mind and feeling for the soul, let us now look at some exercises that you can engage with to translate this new idea into tangible results.

There are five planes of dimensions that work in synergy to create your experience of life. These are the spiritual plane, the emotional or subconscious plane, the mental or rational plane, the bodily or physiological plane, and the material or physical plane. I have grouped the exercises below under these planes to help you stay conscious of which domain of your being you are engaging with when you are practicing a certain exercise.

There is really no rule about which exercise you should practice at what time and how often. The target is for you to get to the point where your life embodies all these practices. You may want to take one at a time, master it, then move to the next in a cumulative manner until you are able to incorporate all of them into your life effortlessly.

SPIRITUAL EXERCISES

The Practice of Faith
In a practical sense, faith is "transcendental awareness", that is, the knowledge of the fundamental principles that orchestrate the world we see. To have faith is to know that what we see, smell, touch, taste, and hear, is not reality, but a phenomenon occurring within reality. It is through this realization that you stop identifying yourself as a body and spontaneously detach from the circumstances that hold you captive. The most practical approach to cultivating faith is to set aside a few minutes each day for spiritual study and meditation.

The Practice of Hope
Hope is the conviction that things will get better. That is a simple truth. From the moment life started on this planet till today, natural disasters, wars, pandemics, depressions, and all crises you can think of have been part and parcel of the human story. But when you connect the dots backward, you will realize that these forces of change have always led us forward and upward. Evolution is an irresistible force. The good news is that it does not need your help. Assure yourself that the best is yet to unfold and that if you just hang on, you will emerge better and stronger. The easiest way to practice

hope is to learn how to be still. Learn to be fully present in this moment.

The Practice of Love

Think about that one person who loves you unconditionally. Create a moment of silence each day in which you can invoke into your present-moment awareness, the best moments you have shared with this person. Immerse yourself in that intimacy and be truly grateful for it. Gradually, it will become easier and easier for you to use this real experience as a trigger for the state of bliss and gratitude. This state of bliss and gratitude is where you want to be most of the time because that is where your power lies.

SOUL EXERCISES

Community

Search within your family and social network and find a handful of people you can build a genuine community with. A true community is a soul circle in which people are their true selves, people feel accepted and unconditionally loved, and people are always looking out for the good of the other person. Although our world is exploding with population increase, people are becoming more and more lonely. Take the lead in building your own community with a purpose in mind. Don't just be a number in a household or neighborhood.

Sharing

Make it a habit to set aside a portion of everything you have so that you can share it with someone in need. The habit of setting aside a portion of everything you have with the intention of giving it away conditions you at a subconscious level to start feeling abundant. And that is the secret; the easiest way to attract what you want is to be the source of it to others.

Service

Having a treasure chest of things you have set aside to share makes it possible for you to share spontaneously. When you meet someone in need, you do not stop and rationalize the cost of helping the person because you already have a bucket for that. It does not have to be anything extraordinary. If you limit your giving to what you have already set aside, you will avoid falling into the trap of either diverting your resources to attend to someone else's need or feeling guilty that you couldn't. Fortunately, it is not just material things that people need. You could serve with your time, your ideas, your companionship, your gifts, and talents, etc.

MENTAL EXERCISES

Revision

Revision is the mental rehearsal of a past event while editing it to conform to your idea of the best version of that story that you can imagine. It is like being in a dream that you are in control of. Take the defining experiences in your life one at a time, and revise them every night on your bed before you fall asleep. Stick with one experience until you have rewritten its emotional script to the degree that your spontaneous memory of the event is the edited version. In the eternity where your conscious states dwell, time does not exist. If you edit your memories, you edit the content of your soul. If you edit the content of your soul, you edit who you are now and who you will become.

Visualization

To visualize is to mentally rehearse a future event the way you want it to turn out. During visualization, you simulate an experience. The good news is that your brain does not know the difference between a simulated experience and an actual experience. When you think of the landlord when you are owing rent, you spontaneously panic, right? That is because you are simulating the "eviction notice" experience and your brain is responding as if it is actually occurring. Conversely, when you daydream of some sweet moment with a loved one, do you realize that your body trembles with the same feeling as if you actually have that person in your arms? That is because your brain thinks you actually do. Decide what you want, then create a mental movie or it and reverse it till it feels like you already have it.

Scripting

Scripting is a powerful tool that engages your spirit, emotions, mind, and body, all at the same time. After your daily meditations, when you are still immersed in the awareness of your transcendent self, take a few moments to write in your journal the image and feel of the best version of yourself that you can imagine.

Affirmations

Let me begin with this warning. Affirmations are a waste of time if all you do is rattle some words that someone has given you to recite. In fact, when you recite affirmations that are not in resonance with your core beliefs and feelings, you do yourself more harm than good because the mental battle throws you into a state of discordance. First, use the spiritual exercises to enter into the awareness of your transcendent reality. Secondly, use the soul exercises to reprogram your subconscious beliefs and feelings. Then, write present-moment affirmations that resonate with that new identity and reality. When you are able to create and recite affirmations that feel true, that is when you can put this great tool to good use.

PHYSIOLOGICAL EXERCISES

Exercise

Find any form of physical exercise that is conducive to your state and that you enjoy doing. Physical exercise increases your blood flow, raising your energy level, and stimulates the secretion of the hormones that orchestrate happiness, healing, growth, digestion, immunity, and overall wellbeing.

Diet

Most people just gulp down anything they can lay their hands on with the sole intention of fighting off the sensation of hunger. That is how our bodies wind up as junkyards, and then we spend a fortune trying to manage weight or treat diseases. Practice intentional nutrition. Remember that your body is a temple that deserves love and attention too.

Select healthy foods, eat at regular intervals and be intentional with your eating. If you remember that "energy flows where attention goes" then it will occur to you that giving your undivided attention to what you are eating actually infuses it with the energy that you are broadcasting at that moment. Eating with the feeling of abundance and gratitude thus becomes a fascinating new way of scripting your future with biological molecules.

Sleep

It is during sleep and relaxation that your body has time to heal, repair, and grow. Sleep and relaxation also switch your body from the sympathetic nervous system to the parasympathetic nervous system. The sympathetic nervous system coordinates your survival mechanisms (stress) while your parasympathetic nervous system coordinates your beingness mechanisms. Setting aside enough time for sleep and relaxation is the cheapest and easiest way to allow your body to heal itself and power you up for effectiveness during your waking hours. More work does not always translate to better results. Focus on being effective, not busy.

PHYSICAL EXERCISES

Nature Immersion
Nature holds the signature vibration of the universe that you may call "The breath of God". Have you noticed that when you are walking in the woods, by a lake, or on the hills you are usually overcome by a feeling of wellbeing, freedom, and expansion? That is because your energy field is being engulfed by the energy field of nature. The result is healing and rejuvenation. You can benefit from this natural healing by practicing it more intentionally and more regularly.

Play
The spiritual masters tell us that the key to the kingdom is in our ability to become like little children. What does it mean to become like a little child? It means to get outside our emotions, get outside our egos, get outside our body-awareness, and just flow. Everyone has a number of hobbies that when they are engaged in, they feel most alive and even out of this world. Find that one thing that you love doing and that when you are doing it, you lose the sense of space and time. Then create time in your schedule to go out and play (practice this hobby) once in a while.

Mirroring
Look at your immediate environment - your living room, your bedroom, your closet, your yard, your office, all the spaces that you have control over. Do the things that surround you mirror the per-

son that you wish to be? Your environment has a subliminal effect on your subconscious. It is a permanent state of hypnosis. Start being aware of your environment. Move things around every now and then. Use decorative flowers and beautiful scents that create a feeling of wellbeing. Surround yourself with photos of your best moments and your heroes. Immerse yourself in wallpapers that mirror your dream life. Take nothing for granted. Create an environment that mirrors your dream self, and you will become that dream.

www.ingramcontent.com/pod-product-compliance
Lightning Source LLC
Chambersburg PA
CBHW061326040426
42444CB00011B/2799